To Patricia — blessings
Pamela Joy Anderson

Pamela Joy Anderson

YOU ARE THE NEEDLE AND I AM THE THREAD

A Memoir of an American Foreign Service Wife

WESTBOW®
PRESS
A DIVISION OF THOMAS NELSON
& ZONDERVAN

Only be careful, and watch yourselves closely so that you do not forget the things your eyes have seen or let them fade from your heart as long as you live. Teach them to your children and to their children after them. (Deuteronomy 4:9 Women's Devotional Bible New International Version)

For Tim, who believed in me, and without whom this life and this book would not have been possible.

Prologue

"O God, I am Mustafah the tailor and I work at the shop of Muhammad. The whole day long I sit and pull the needle and the thread through the cloth. O God, you are the needle and I am the thread. I am attached to you and I follow you. When the thread tries to slip away from the needle it becomes tangled and must be cut so that it can be put back in the right place. O God, help me to follow you wherever you may lead me. For I am really only Mustafah the tailor and I work at the shop of Muhammad on the great square."

A prayer by Mustafah, a Muslim convert to Christianity

This prayer resonates deep within me. Oh, how I feel like Mustafah the tailor as I sit and contemplate the cloth of our life as Christians in the Islamic world over a period of 22 years during my husband's Foreign Service postings on three continents. As an inveterate quilter myself and now officially retired from teaching, I still pull the needle and thread through the quilt, and I have more time to sit and contemplate the tapestry God is forming from my tangled threads. I am chagrined that it's taken me more than thirty years to fully comprehend that God is the needle and I am the thread, and when I slip away from Him, I get myself all tangled up and my strands must be cut so I can be put back in the right place. Like Mustafah, I try to follow God, but I know that I am only a small stitch in the larger tapestry of life that He is creating thread by thread.

Our tapestry started to take shape back in Clarkston, Washington in 1986, but it later took us all over the Islamic world with my husband's job with the U.S. Agency for International Development (USAID), the development assistance arm of the U.S. Government, first in Pakistan, then Egypt, back to the U.S. in Washington, D.C., then out to Bangladesh, Afghanistan, and lastly, Indonesia.

More than thirty years ago as a relatively new Christian, I wondered to myself, "How does God communicate with people? How does He talk to me and how can I talk to Him?" I had read numerous stories that told about people hearing voices, seeing visions, or having their prayers miraculously answered. I was familiar with the biblical stories of Moses and the Burning Bush, the parting of the Red Sea, and the angel's visit to the Virgin Mary, among others. After pondering these stories, several questions still remained: Does God perform miracles today, or were

Tim have any experience in international development and relief work? No. Did Tim speak Spanish? No. Did Tim have experience as an office administrator? No. Despite these negatives, both the interviewer and Tim felt very positive about the interview and he was hired as the administrator for Northwest Medical Teams. I also found work, a job with the Oregon State Legislature.

More than thirty years have passed since that time in Washington and Oregon, and much has happened. Most importantly, we witnessed a rekindling of our spirits as new opportunities led us overseas. Looking back, we agree there was no way we could have planned the path our lives would take. We see how God has orchestrated the events of our lives and how He has shaped us. It hasn't always been comfortable or easy, but based on our past experiences, we would much rather have God in charge than to rely solely on ourselves. We have seen how little seemingly innocuous things like songs on the radio, poems, or a comforting word could have come only from God. We no longer believe in coincidence. We have been comforted by angels, who, themselves, may have been unaware that they were doing God's bidding. Were these signs and answers to prayers miraculous? At first glance, they didn't appear to be, but then, perhaps subtlety plays a part in God's mysterious ways.

In Salem, Oregon, Tim's restlessness continued and like the desert nomad described by the British explorer and travel writer, Sir Wilfred Thesiger, he sensed a calling to respond to the yearning within him. Although the nomad is compelled to follow the call of the desert, Tim's call was less defined, but it was no less insistent. He felt the urge to do something, but he didn't yet know what that something was. According to Thesiger, who explored the Empty Quarter in Arabia, the nomad "will carry, however faint, the imprint of the desert, the brand which marks the nomad; and he will have the yearning to return, weak or insistent according to his nature." At the time, I lamented Tim's larger mustard seed of faith that had been apportioned to him and my own rather small one. In looking back, there were only two things I felt certain of at that time: we would never settle down in a permanent place because of Tim's restless nature, and we would never have the American Dream as it's usually defined. If Tim were a ship on the sea of adventure, I was the ballast of his vessel, which provided the stability to our course.

Around this time, Tim felt a calling to take the summer off and to attend classes at the Center for World Missions in southern California even though he would have to leave his job with Northwest Medical Teams to do so. I had a short-term teaching job as the coordinator and teacher for a Japanese home-stay program through our church, so we had a small amount of money coming in. I had completed most of the coursework for my Master's degree in Teaching English as a Second Language (TESL), but I had not yet completed the thesis.

Tim applied to the Center for World Missions and was accepted in their summer program. While enrolled and reading one of his textbooks at the Center, he came across an article written by a man named Cleo, who lived in nearby Monrovia, California. The article recounted Cleo's experiences and outlined several corollaries acquired after a lifetime of working as a Christian layman in the field of international development. Here are some of his conclusions after a 17-year career with USAID: 1. The synthesis of community development and evangelism is biblical. 2. Evangelism and community development are co-forces for bringing about the more abundant life that Jesus talks about. 3. Development is the logical reaction of an informed Christian to the physical needs of a desperately needy world.

On an internal prompting, Tim called Cleo to ask if they could meet, to which Cleo kindly agreed. One of the burning questions Tim had was whether Christian faith and government service were compatible. In the ensuing discussion Tim was reassured that by working in such areas as education, health, job training, and disaster relief and food security, he would be meeting the needs of the whole man. Cleo also gave Tim some well-thought-out advice concerning his own life with USAID: be flexible; be aware that what you expect to occur will most likely not occur; roll with the punches; be prepared to make ad hoc decisions; be able to assess a situation and make a decision; join a local church as soon as possible; let the spirit of the Lord lead. Cleo went on to state that too few Christians were willing to take personal chances for God's Kingdom. One telling comment was formed as a question – "Why does the Devil attract risk takers and our Lord timid disciples?"

While Tim was still at the Center for World Missions, I received a call in Salem, Oregon from USAID in Washington, D.C. asking me if Tim was coming to the interview because he hadn't replied to the interview request. I was dumbfounded. What interview? Where? Why didn't he tell me about this? This was the first time I had heard about any interview. As it turned out, Tim had sent a resume several years earlier to USAID but had forgotten about it. Apparently, someone had kept the resume buried in his desk drawer just in case the agency would need someone with Tim's commodities background. It was at this time that a hiring window had opened up within USAID for Commodity Management Officers. Tim's experience working for an international agricultural cooperative buying and selling peas, beans, and lentils and dealing in matters of logistics; our short stint in the Peace Corps; and his six years as a grain trader fit the bill. It was only later in looking back that we recognized God's serendipity in this series of events.

Tim was eager to go to Washington for the interview, but USAID would not help cover the transportation or the lodging costs. Again, God's hand was in the experience because an anonymous donor in our church provided a portion of the expenses, most likely our pastor, Jack, and his wife, Beve, and the Board of Directors of Northwest Medical Teams provided another portion to allow Tim to follow his dream and fly to Washington, D.C for the interview. In looking back, we marvel at the generosity of spirit that would allow the Board of Directors of Northwest Medical Teams to encourage one of their employees to apply for another position and even help pay for the cost!

After an extensive interview process, Tim was hired, and he flew back to D.C. to begin the year-long training program. The boys and I stayed back in Salem so I could finish the coursework for my Master's degree and the boys could finish half a year of school in Salem. We were eager to start on this new adventure because of the possibility that Tim's job would lead us all over the world. It was a dream that had come true. I've always said that Tim was born 100 years too late and on the wrong continent. He would have made a wonderful British colonial administrator, and it turned out that those administrative skills made for a well-equipped USAID officer. My background in teaching ESL was also fortuitous, and it made for a very portable career to have in following my husband around the world. We were also delighted to discover upon entering USAID that we found people of like minds, those who were interested in a larger world view; where once we had felt like square pegs in round holes, we now felt like we finally fit the mold. We wondered whether God had sent divine restlessness to Tim to direct him to the path we ultimately followed.

Joining USAID was such a big adventure, and it would take us so far from home…We weren't certain of our future at the time, but we felt this was an opportunity we couldn't pass up. We hadn't read any of the writings of Soren Kierkegaard, the Danish philosopher and theologian, but our thoughts mirrored his thoughts in the following quote: "To dare is to lose one's footing momentarily. Not to dare is to lose oneself."

The next hurdle was getting the family back to Washington, D.C., where Tim would start his year-long training program before being posted overseas. He flew back to D.C. to begin training and the boys and I stayed in Salem to prepare for the move. Since USAID would not pay for the domestic shipment of a vehicle, he decided that the Thanksgiving break would give him the opportunity to fly back to Oregon after he finished work on Wednesday in D.C. and to drive our vehicle from Oregon across country to Washington, D.C. in time to report back to work on Monday. Neither of us wanted me to drive the car through the snowy Midwest with our two young sons ages six and eight. We both knew we couldn't sell our old car in Oregon and buy another in Washington, D.C. to replace it because we had done our homework and found that the cost of living in D.C. was much higher than in Oregon.

My mom and I met Tim at the Portland airport at midnight on Wednesday, the day before Thanksgiving. We came armed with two apple pies my mom had baked (she always said she'd be remembered for her apple pies) and a six-pack of Jolt, a high-caffeine soft drink. The Jolt was to keep Tim awake on the long drive, and the pies were for him to barter for car repair in case our ancient car broke down in the middle of nowhere. Although he has many fine qualities, car repair is not one of them.

Tim remembers driving all that night and into the next day listening to talk radio and keeping the windows open for fresh air to keep him awake. His goal was to drive as far as he could and keep ahead of the snow storms that dogged his path. Local radio stations would report one road closing after another as soon as Tim had crossed each mountain pass in the road. My mom was convinced he was able to escape the brunt of the snowstorms and keep driving because we had both prayed him across the country. It was in Nebraska where he first stopped for the night, and somewhere in the middle of the Plains in a nondescript diner where he enjoyed a leftover Thanksgiving dinner, albeit a day late. Tim finally rolled into a hotel in Falls Church, Virginia after 2 ½ days of driving.

In Virginia, he kept reading the local papers to search for rental houses but discovered that by the time he found a prospective house, it had already been rented. He finally found one, a cute little cracker box house in Falls Church kitty corner from Thomas Jefferson Elementary School, where the boys could walk to school. We called it the Little House on the Big Lot. The boys and I flew into D.C. on December 17 and settled into our new home. The driver of the van that held all our worldly goods called on Christmas Eve and asked if we'd like him to deliver our stuff.

We were ecstatic as we went through all our boxes and un-wrapped our belongings to the accompaniment of Christmas carols and the gentle falling of big flakes of snow. It was a magical Christmas full of excitement and anticipation. We were starting a new chapter in our lives.

The year of training in D.C. passed quickly with Tim's Spanish language course and his job-specific training as an International Development Intern. I found work teaching ESL at night in the Fairfax County Adult and Community Education program. We made the most of our time in Virginia that year exploring Civil War battlefields, the National Zoo, the Smithsonian museums, and Mary Stiles Riley Library, which even loaned video tapes!

One enduring image I have of Tim that year in Washington was him trudging off to the bus with his headphones glued to his ears. Language study did not come easily to him, and it was only through perseverance that he was able to pass the Spanish language test after 22 weeks of study with a 2/2 for listening and speaking as well as reading and writing. We had hoped that with his language study we would be sent to a Spanish-speaking post, but that was not meant to be. We learned we would be sent to Pakistan, and we immediately started reading all we could to help prepare ourselves for our future posting. Maybe we would encounter some mythical Spanish-speaking community in the wilds of Pakistan so he could use his Spanish. We also enrolled in various classes at the Foreign Service Institute in Arlington, Virginia to learn all we could about our new life.

Some well-meaning friends and family questioned our plans to live in Pakistan and asked whether we were frightened to be moving to such a dangerous part of the world. Our response at the time was, "Don't you think that God's presence is everywhere and not just in the U.S.?"

One memorable class was a required three-day Security Training class where we had danger, danger, danger pounded into our heads while we learned how to escape from a burning building; how to evade surveillance; how to use the skills of counter surveillance to be alert and observe our surroundings at all times; how to survive if we were taken hostage; and how to survive a plane hijacking or plane crash. At the end of the three-day period I remember turning to Tim and asking him if we really wanted to go to Pakistan. What had we gotten ourselves into? We both felt a little doubtful at the time, and we realized only after a few months in Pakistan that we were still operating in the "orange alert" mode and needed to come down from our hyper vigilance.

Chapter One • Pakistan

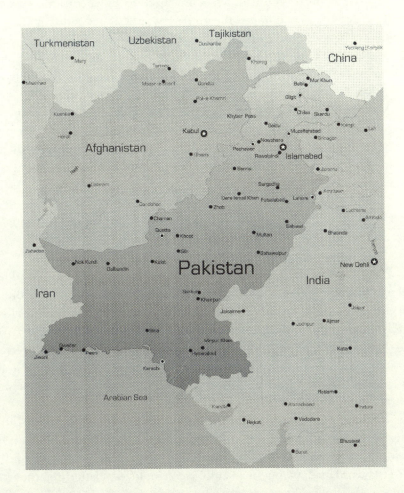

*O God, help me to follow you wherever you may lead me...*Our first overseas assignment with USAID was to Islamabad, Pakistan from 1989 to 1993. We arrived one evening and were met by Tim's new boss, Steve, who took us to our duplex in the sector, F7. Tim and I remember doing a high-five after wandering throughout the cavernous home that was now ours. As most Pakistani families live in multiple-family units, houses can be quite large and many in Islamabad consist of at least five bedrooms. Ours had five bedrooms and four bathrooms. It was quite a change from our two-bedroom, one bath cracker box home in Falls Church. Later that night exhausted as we prepared for bed, we heard the sounds of gunfire erupt nearby, and we peered anxiously over the edge of the second floor balcony.

1

We couldn't believe our bad luck to be experiencing a shootout or a coup on our first night in-country. We slunk back to our bedrooms through the darkened house and hoped the gunfire would stop. Gradually the pop, pop, pop lessened and we drifted off to sleep. We learned the next day that our neighbors had merely been celebrating the election of Benazir Bhutto as Prime Minister by shooting their Kalashnikovs into the air. Welcome to Pakistan!

Most first assignments, or postings, are the most intense, and I soon discovered that Pakistan and I had a love/hate relationship, primarily because I found it difficult being a western woman in an Islamic society so different from our own. The following story relates my attempts at learning how to be a chameleon in our new life.

Memsahib

I had a lot to learn about living overseas. I arrived in Islamabad as a relative ingénue with my husband and two small boys for our first Foreign Service assignment. Like most American newcomers to overseas life, I was determined to put my best foot forward. Life had taught me that if you searched for the best in everyone, you usually found it. The converse is also true. So, I approached our Foreign Service life full of goodwill and high expectations. I learned later that I had a lot to learn about being a memsahib.

The word, memsahib, as it is used in Pakistan, is fraught with meaning. Put simply, it confers honor to an older Pakistani or a foreign woman, but then nothing is as simple as it looks. Memsahib is often interchangeable with the word madam, but in an employer/employee relationship the word conveys a host of privileges and accompanying duties. I was not sure I liked the word memsahib.

I had never been comfortable with the word servant either. I was told that in Islamabad, most families hired at least one, if not several, servants to clean and take care of the expansive houses, most of them large enough to accommodate several generations under one roof. Division of labor was one carry-over from the Indian caste system. I resigned myself to the inevitability of having one servant, a jack-of-all-trades, but I vowed to refer to that person as our household help.

Somehow word gets out that a new family is in town, and potential servants miraculously appear, as if guided by radar. Altaf was the first person to show up at our doorstep, chits in hand, eager to do whatever was asked of him. That should have tipped me off right there.

Altaf's most noticeable mannerism was his willingness. He was obsequious in the way he presented himself, but he was clean, his English was passable, and his references indicated he was a hard worker. He also reminded me of a weasel the way his eyes darted back and forth as I conducted the interview, but I needed someone, and from the way Altaf talked, he was desperate. So, he got the job. That was my first mistake. For a woman who never bought anything until she had checked out every option, the decision seemed hasty, but then, I was new at hiring household help.

"Altaf, are you boiling and filtering the water the way that you are supposed to?

"Yes, memsahib."

"Altaf, are you cleaning and soaking the fruits and vegetables like I asked you to?"

"Yes, memsahib."

I preferred a hands-off style of management. I knew some cooks had a proprietary attitude toward the kitchen and considered it their sole domain, so I left Altaf alone. That was my second mistake.

That first month in Islamabad was a difficult one for my family and me. Stomach problems plagued us all, and it seemed like I was forever trotting to the Health Unit with our brown paper bags of stool samples in hand. The Health Unit diagnosed our family's problems as a grab-bag of amoebic dysentery, shigella, and giardiasis. That first month I lost ten pounds. When I asked Altaf about his personal hygiene and food preparation, he replied, "No problem, memsahib. Stomach always trouble new people until you here long time."

Even before Altaf's grace period was half over, he began asking for more wages and perks. "I poor man and you rich. I needing more money. Other memsahibs giving shoes and uniforms."

As I had already expended more than a month's salary on equipping the servant's quarters with a bed and bedding, towels, a gas stove and cookware, I was starting to think that Altaf was taking advantage of me.

Meanwhile, I was also having problems with Safdar, our mali/sweeper (gardener). Safdar appeared at the door one day recommended by Altaf. He was an older man with a young wife and several children to support. He was a Christian, unlike the other servants and guards at our duplex. He, too, was a poor man who showed up for work in shoes several sizes too big for him. They clip-clopped as he walked and made blisters on his heels. His shalwar kurta, hiked halfway to his knees, was threadbare and usually torn, a fact he routinely pointed out to me. I gave him money for new shoes and 300 rupees for a new shalwar kurta not knowing that the going price for a ready-made shalwar kurta was 125 rupees at Aabpara Market. He wore his shoes to work once and returned from the market to show me the fine material he had bought with the rupees I gave him. I never saw his new outfit.

Safdar's work was adequate, and for the first month he was diligent in weeding the flower beds and pruning the bushes. He would occasionally knock at the door with a bouquet of fresh-cut flowers to present to me.

Working in the garden was one of my connections to home. I loved to grub in the dirt and found that the physical labor of gardening helped me work through some of the tensions I was experiencing in our new post. My favorite flower is the tulip, which to me symbolized permanence. Because of our family's many moves, I never felt quite settled until I had been in one place at least three seasons – long enough so that I could plant tulip bulbs in the fall and watch them come up in the spring. I wanted that same permanence in Islamabad. Outside the wall at the front of the property was a bare patch of earth just aching for some color. I eyed the bare ground with the intent of planting a bed of bright, perky tulips.

I pored over the Michigan Bulb Company's glossy brochures and picked out several varieties of bulbs in enough quantities to carpet the front area. The only problem in sending off the order was determining the correct planting zone according to the chart depicting U.S. climates. I took a stab at the correct zone, indicated the southern tier on the chart, and sent off the order form.

I waited and waited and grew more anxious for my bulbs to arrive as the weather turned colder. In the meantime, I decided to prepare the ground for planting. Because the soil was clay-like and rock hard, I got out the pickaxe and shovel to attack the dirt. Soon I had worked up a sweat and had also attracted a crowd of interested bystanders. Some passersby almost fell off their bicycles, their heads swiveling 180 degrees in an attempt to stare at me as they moved down the street. Apparently, they had never seen a memsahib sweat.

I enlisted the help of my husband who worked over the clumps of soil with the hand-pushed Rototiller. As we worked, we both noticed Mohammed Siddique, our chowkidar (guard), getting increasingly uncomfortable. He, too, had not seen a sahib and memsahib do physical labor. The passersby seemed to be passing judgment on Mohammed Siddique, who stood idly by at his guard post while his employers worked like field hands. Soon he was working alongside us, breaking up the bigger clumps with a shovel.

Finally, the package from the Michigan Bulb Company arrived, but instead of the expected tulip bulbs, the package contained a refund check and a consolation prize of a few Sweet William roots. The letter indicated that the tulip planting season in our area had already passed, and they were refunding our money. It wasn't until much later that I found that bulbs could be bought from the nurseries out by Rawal Lake near Rawalpindi.

Everything was going fine until one day I came home to find our back yard, a postage stamp piece of grass, half denuded.

"What in the world are you doing, Safdar?"

"Me taking out bad grass, memsahib," Safdar replied.

"What's the difference between good grass and bad grass?" I asked. I looked, but I couldn't find any evidence of crab grass, the only "bad" grass that I could identify. With great difficulty, I convinced Safdar to stop pulling the bad grass out, for I feared our backyard would become a sea of mud once the rainy season started. Safdar sullenly did as he was told.

I returned to the house one afternoon to find the beautiful rose bushes that had lined the driveway were now two-inch stumps. "What did you do to my beautiful rose bushes, Safdar?" I demanded.

"Important cut roses before spring so next year strong," Safdar said. I was horrified at the mutilation of our beautiful rose bushes and none too happy with Safdar for doing it.

About this same time, Altaf's demands became more insistent. His cooking was terrible, and in addition, the family was all still sick. Altaf was the only cook I knew who could ruin Jello. He had also demolished several pairs of pants, leaving large bleach marks on them.

I obtained a copy of the Community Liaison Office's guide to food and water preparation, which was illustrated and written in both English and Urdu. I presented the booklet to Altaf, who immediately put it in the kitchen drawer.

Because everyone in the family was still complaining of stomach problems, I became more vigilant in supervising Altaf. One day I caught him cleaning the fruits and vegetables improperly with just tap water. That was the final straw.

"Altaf, why aren't you cleaning the vegetables properly? Where is the booklet I gave you?"

"But memsahib, I cleaning vegetables good. Book here in drawer," Altaf defended himself by pulling out the drawer and pointing to the booklet.

Finally it dawned on me. I was asking the wrong types of questions. I should never have asked yes/no questions, for Pakistanis are reluctant to tell a foreigner no. Even if they don't know the answer, they will give you some sort of answer, the one they think you want to hear. For Pakistanis, the relationship between people is more important than what we in the West call truth value.

It turned out that Altaf could not read or write in Urdu or English, but I had never asked for a demonstration of his reading ability. To Altaf, a book in the drawer was the same as knowledge in the head.

It was time to let Altaf go. He pleaded for another chance, saying that he would do better next time and he really needed the job. I stood my ground and ordered him and his belongings out of the servant's quarters by the next morning. I dreaded the inspection of his quarters, but I was convinced the family was better off without Altaf. Who cared more about our family's health than me?

I noticed that the bedding and the cookware had disappeared into Altaf's belongings that were strapped on top of the black and white taxi. I was willing to let those items go in exchange for no confrontation.

"I need our key before I can pay you your salary, Altaf."

"Sorry, memsahib. I no have key. Key lost."

"All right, Altaf. When you find our key, I will find your salary." And with those words, I stepped into the house and locked the door.

Five minutes passed before there was a knock on the door. Altaf stood there, the key in his hand and a defiant look on his face. He said that it was a miracle he had found the key. I paid Altaf the money I owed him but would not give him a recommendation. I was learning.

For the next nine months, I did the work myself. I swept and mopped what seemed like miles of marble floors, and I boiled and filtered oceans of water. What bothered me the most after spending the whole afternoon in preparation for dinner, was to then spend hours washing the dishes. Mohammed Siddique, our chowkidar, had just the answer to our problem.

Mohammed Siddique was a middle-aged Kashmiri man who had retired from the army but was supplementing his pension by being a guard. He had the kindest brown eyes I had ever seen. He also had a large indentation in his forehead, probably from some skirmish in Kashmir. We communicated by hand signals and smiles, and somehow, it worked.

One day, Mohammed Siddique approached me with a proposition. He would do the evening dishes for us after his shift was over in exchange for being able to live in the now-vacant servant's quarters. The idea was a godsend, which relieved me of an irksome chore and provided Mohammed Siddique with quarters at very little expense to him. He was true to his word, and every evening could be found standing barefoot next to the sink, with soapsuds halfway up to his elbows. The situation worked well for all of us.

Spring came and with it came confirmation that Safdar did know what he was doing after all. Our experimental grass plot in the backyard showed the half that had been plucked of "bad" grass was now bright green and luxurious. The other half showed grass that was spotty and lackluster. The rose bushes sprouted new growth and by fall would be back to their original height. The best part was that the buds were well formed and numerous, promising beautiful blooms come summer time. Calendula and Cosmos bloomed bright yellow, orange, and pink in front of the wall where the tulips would have been planted.

I smiled to myself and reflected on the word, memsahib. Yes, I still had much to learn.

§

After nine months of doing my own housecleaning as well as food shopping and preparation, I was ready to try hiring another cook bearer. We were in luck. Our friends next door, the Swifts, on the other side of the duplex, had a wonderful cook bearer named Suleiman. Suleiman was an older man who had been trained by a British memsahib and was a gourmet cook. Suleiman had a friend, Ali, from Abbottabad who was looking for work. We hired Ali, and he turned out to be a trusted employee for three years.

Ali was an older man also, probably close to 60 years of age. He had worked for British memsahibs and had wonderful cooking skills. Ali was the sole source of income for his family of three sons, their wives, and their children, all of whom still lived in Abbottabad. Although Ali was a wonder in the kitchen, he could not read recipes because he had never learned to read in English. Everything he cooked or baked had to be memorized. I tried to teach him how to read and write, but after several months Ali gave up. He got stuck near the beginning of the alphabet with the letters "e" and "f." He had the firm belief that he was too old to learn and no amount of patience or talk could dissuade him of that belief. His ideas about age and education were one of the areas where our two cultures clashed.

Over time we picked up another servant, a dhobi (laundryman), who would work part-time and do the ironing. I still preferred to do the wash myself. My resolve to have just one servant, a jack-of-all-trades, dissolved in the pressure to conform to Pakistani society, which still held to the firm belief of division of labor, so all in all, towards the end of our posting we had a full-time cook bearer (cook and cleaner), a full-time chowkidar (guard), a part-time mali (gardener), and a part-time dhobi.

Although we paid our household help well and even bought health insurance for Ali, our employees had difficulty making their salaries stretch from month to month. Because of this, I instituted a social security system for the four of them and set aside 10% of my salary each month (in rupees), gained from my part-time contract jobs, which would be divided among them when we left for our next posting. This money would tide them over until they could find new employment following our departure from Pakistan. They could also borrow against their next month's salary, and a percentage of the amount borrowed would be docked from each month's wages until their small loan was repaid. As their employer, I became responsible for all of their needs, and we ended up paying for a varicose vein operation for Ali. I also served as an informal arbiter of disputes, a nurse who administered common medicines and patched up cuts and abrasions, and a banker. It was a lot of responsibility for my age and I felt like I had six children rather than two; this unwritten social contract weighed heavily on me.

When I think back to our four years in Pakistan, my mind is flooded with vivid memories of my encounters with the culture and the expectations imposed upon me as a western woman. Because of the strictures of purdah, the Islamic practice of secluding women in their home away from the stares of strange men, most of the people I would see on the street were male. There was such an imbalance of the sexes represented on the streets of Islamabad and every other city in Pakistan that one would assume Mother Nature had made a grievous error in apportioning the sexes to produce 98% males and 2% females. Being surrounded by men had a disconcerting effect on me. It didn't take me long to figure out that the American practice of looking people in the eye wouldn't work in Pakistan because a direct look at a stranger on the street could be construed as a come-on, and I would be thought of as a hussy at best. I spent four years with my eyes glued to the ground.

I quickly learned I was more comfortable wearing shalwar kameez, the loose, baggy pantaloon bottoms and long tunic top, preferably one that covered my upper arms, and I wore long-sleeved kameezes even in the hottest weather. I learned how to expertly flip the dupatta, the long decorative scarf, over my shoulders in an effort to conceal my breasts. Tight shalwar kameezes were frowned upon because they showed the female form; the baggier the outfit the better. Showing even a tiny bit of cleavage was scandalous, and living in Pakistan warped my sense of dressing and style. It certainly warped my sense of who I was as a woman. I was ever vigilant to button up and do the bend over test to make sure I wasn't showing anything I shouldn't be showing.

I was aware that a woman who flaunted the norms of correct female conduct could easily be stoned or worse. The daily newspapers recounted stories of women who had burned to death in unexplained kitchen fires in honor killings or had had acid thrown in their faces by an incensed husband or father. Because the family's honor resided in the chastity of the women, even an accusation of infidelity was cause for the killing of a daughter or wife to avenge the male family members' honor. It seemed to me that women were seen as baby makers and valued slightly above cattle, to be bought or sold in marriage. When a daughter was born, it was a time to mourn not to celebrate, especially if there were already several daughters in the family. A daughter was seen as another mouth to feed until she became of marriageable age, perhaps 13 or 14, at which time she would go to the husband's family and leave her birth family forever.

Admittedly, we were not able to effectively cross the cultural barriers that prevented us from becoming close friends with any Pakistanis, so perhaps my perceptions were somewhat skewed. Walled compounds surrounding houses did not make for neighborly relations, and the relationships we formed at work were cordial but not close. Americans were not particularly well liked because of international tensions related to the American Pressler Amendment, which stated that if our government could not verify the country receiving development assistance was not pursuing weapons-related nuclear ambitions, it would have its development assistance cut off. Two years after we arrived in Pakistan, Tim as a Commodity Management and Procurement Officer, had to deal with closing programs down because USAID was forced to reduce its in-country presence on account of the Pressler Amendment.

As we read the local papers, primarily *The Dawn*, we learned about Pakistan's nuclear race with India, and it became clear to us that Pakistan felt very much like an underdog because of its smaller population and its perceived smaller stockpile of arms, both conventional and nuclear. Pakistan felt both outgunned and outmanned. Pakistan and India were still skirmishing over the contested territory of Kashmir, which both countries claimed. The disputes over territory were formed by Partition in 1947, and they continue today.

We were into our fourth year at post before I was presented with a view that slightly changed my perception of girls and women. I remember sitting in one of the waiting lounges in the Karachi airport when I saw a father dandling his young daughter on his knee. He held her and spoke to her so lovingly I was forced to reconsider my perception of the value of females in Pakistan. It seemed sad, however, that it had taken three years to reveal that loving image of a father to his young daughter.

Despite the negative view towards women in general, foreign women were a different matter. We foreign women seemed to be treated as honorary men and were often given places of honor at gatherings. There seemed to be a third sex, "the other," and it helped to explain how a country such as Pakistan which discriminates against 50% of its population could elect a woman as Prime Minister. I came to the conclusion that Benazir Bhutto was not just a woman; she was Zulfikar Ali Bhutto's daughter with all the weight of a wealthy feudal ruling family and an Oxford education behind her.

The segregation of the sexes in Pakistan took a while to get used to. We heard from our cook bearer, Ali, that the mother of Taimur, the next-door neighbor boy our boys climbed trees with, had died in London after a bout with cancer. Ali informed us that the respectful thing to do was to attend the memorial gathering. We could see from our bedroom window the shamiana, the colorful appliqued tent raised in the front yard of our neighbors' house in preparation for the event. On the chosen day, Ali, as our cross-cultural interpreter, shepherded us next door to pay our respects. I was quickly whisked inside, where I was shown to the living room, which was lined with women sitting in chairs. Tim was relegated to the group of men gathered under the shamiana.

I was the only foreign woman present, so I took a seat next to a kindly looking older Pakistani woman. It was at this point that I felt most American. I noticed no one in the room was talking, but as an American, I felt the need to fill the empty silence with words – something, anything to overcome my discomfort. After a half hour or so of prattling to the woman sitting next to me, I became quiet and endured the next 1 ½ hours in silence. I learned later that to Pakistanis, the most important aspect of expressing condolences to someone grieving is your presence. Words were not needed.

I remember our first introduction to grocery shopping in Islamabad when we were taken to the Covered Market. The market was arranged with a variety of small shops encircling a center of fruit and vegetable stalls, each with a mound of beautifully arranged pyramids of oranges, apples, and vegetables of all kinds. As it was late summer when we first arrived in Islamabad, the weather was quite sultry, and the configuration of the market didn't allow for much cross ventilation, so the smells of the overripe fruit and the chicken detritus in the meat areas were quite overpowering. I saw a beautifully stacked pyramid of oranges that seemed to have been studded with cloves. "How lovely," I thought. "They've pre-studded the oranges." On closer inspection, the "cloves" turned out to be flies.

One could walk up to the meat vendor, point to a chicken in a wooden crate, and then the merchant would quickly dispatch the chicken and have it plucked and ready to go in a matter of minutes. Some clever entrepreneur also cottoned onto the idea that Americans like to cook turkey for their Thanksgiving dinner, so for a few months of the year, you would see live turkeys strutting their stuff around the market.

It was in Islamabad that I learned how to cut up a chicken, thanks to my Joy of Cooking cookbook. I also learned to only buy seafood during the months that contained an "r" in them. This was the rule according to a kindly older butcher from Abbottabad who owned a meat market in Jinnah Supermarket. His shop was a good source for quality meat, and you could ask him which cut of beef you would need for any dish you were planning to cook. Pork, of course, was not available due to the Islamic belief that pigs were unclean animals.

For fresh produce, I would often go to Jinnah Supermarket, the closest market to our home, to one of the fruit and vegetable vendors. One day I bought two kilos of potatoes only to get them home and find every single one was either rotten or had a shovel mark in it. I immediately returned to Jinnah to complain to the vendor and told him if he would give me good produce I would be a loyal customer and buy my produce only from him. I think he had the belief that Pakistani customers were more particular about their produce, and he could fob off his bad stuff on his unsuspecting American customers. By confronting this vendor, I assured myself of good-quality produce thereafter, but I realized that confrontations such as those were part of my negative feelings toward Pakistanis and their culture,

11

and I would have to gird myself for battle whenever I encountered a new vendor. Bargaining didn't come naturally for me, and it was only months later that I took the grocery shopping process more lightheartedly and began to enjoy it.

I enjoyed sewing, and it was fascinating to visit the fabric shops in Aabpara Market, where fabrics of all kinds and colors could be bought. What I found most interesting was the array of colors in the fabrics, color combinations that I wouldn't normally see in the U.S.: candy-apple green, fire-engine orange, and baby blue for example. These colors were meant to showcase the darker skin and eye color of Pakistani women, but they didn't necessarily highlight my blond hair and fair coloring. Rumors among the American expat women said that I should avoid one of the largest shops in Aabpara Market, for one of their salesmen had a habit of getting "touchy feely" with his western customers whenever he unrolled a bolt of fabric and held it up under the woman's chin. Sure enough, the rumors were correct as I felt Mr. Touchy Feely's hand brush against my breast, and I avoided his shop from then on.

Our leased houses came equipped with sturdy and functional furniture (I called it early motel), and I had the pleasure of selecting fabrics to upholster the chairs and sofas as well as the windows. There was a list of approved tailors who would come to the house to measure the furniture and windows to give you an estimate of the meters of fabric needed. I remember feeling overwhelmed to know that I would have to purchase 174 meters of fabric to cover the chairs, sofas, and the windows of our two-story duplex. It was a daunting task, and I set about gathering fabric swatches to show to Tim. My goal was to select sturdy fabrics in colors that would hold up to two rambunctious boys, and for the most part, my selections were good. I was disappointed with the plush fabric I selected for the living room couch, however, and I complained to my next door neighbor, Fran, about the color, which in the store looked a steel blue but at home looked gray. It was too late to take the fabric back because it had already been cut. Fran's advice was, "You'll get used to it."

Ultimately, I did get used to the expanse of gray on our early motel sofa, and I also got used to seeing the tailor sit cross-legged on our living room floor with his sewing machine and lengths of fabric arrayed before him. Miraculously, a month later our furniture and windows were fully covered but not without one major glitch. Our tailor was savvy enough to know we were newcomers, and when he asked me if I wanted full pleats in the draperies, of course I said yes. It was only later when presented with a bill that was several hundred dollars larger than the allotted amount USAID would pay for labor that I discovered my naiveté came with a price: USAID would pay for two-inch pleats, not the three-inch pleats the tailor had already made.

It was in Pakistan where we were disabused of the idea that if you were in trouble to go to the police. In the U.S., children are taught that a policeman can be trusted, but in Pakistan it was quite different. Because the police are paid such paltry salaries, they're often on the take to supplement their income and if you're in trouble, bribes are de rigueur.

To me, Pakistani society at the corporate level seemed joyless. I rarely saw smiles on the faces of the people I saw on the streets, and it seemed that Islam had too many "thou shalt nots." The strict segregation of the sexes also meant that normal female activities such as shopping would be done by the men, and it always seemed strange to see a man shopping for his wife's bras in the Covered Market, for example. I was also taken aback to see men walking along holding each other's pinky finger. I learned this was a sign of close male friendship and had no homosexual overtones, but it took me a long time to get used to that sight. Because there could be no public physical contact between the sexes, Tim and I had to learn not to hold hands while walking in the market or on the streets.

Pakistan's low level of literacy in addition to its high level of poverty had an impact on all areas of life. At the time we lived there, the overall percentage of people who were literate was 25%. This lack of literacy affected the general hygiene in the country, despite the fact that most Muslims pray five times a day and do their ablutions prior to their prayers. It was difficult for people to understand germ theory, and they thought if they couldn't see anything on their hands, they must be clean. It was also a common sight to see men squatting by the side of the road with the flap of their kurta raised so they could pee in the ditch. Toilet tissue was not widely used – the left hand was reserved for that function. Public restrooms were non-existent, and over the course of four years, I learned how to dehydrate myself in order to avoid urinating. Oh how I wished I had been born with male plumbing.

Most expats suffered from recurring intestinal parasites, and some even came to use their tummy troubles as a form of weight management. Islamabad was the only post where the Regional Medical Officer outlawed salads and recommended people eat only cooked foods and fruits that could be peeled. Apparently, it is almost impossible to prevent parasites and bacteria from wicking up the veins of a lettuce leaf.

The first winter was difficult for the family because both boys developed asthma that year. Their asthma was brought on by the fact that Islamabad was located at the base of the Margalla Hills, the foothills of the Himalayas, and the winter smog blanketed the city. Its position just a few miles north of Rawalpindi, an industrialized area, made matters worse. The air quality was further exacerbated by the small fires the guards would light to keep themselves warm at night during their watch and the smoke that emanated from the refugee camps, which housed millions of refugees who were also lighting fires to keep themselves warm.

Our family's air quality was also affected by our neighbor's burning of their garbage, which they burned close to their opposite perimeter wall. Unfortunately for us, the wall separated our property from theirs, and the smoke wafted directly into our air conditioning and heating unit, which spread it throughout the house. It's such a frantic feeling to watch your child struggle to draw a breath, and as parents, we discovered there's not a more wonderful sight in the world than seeing the doctor come through the front door with his black bag in hand. The doctor made house calls, something unheard of in the U.S. He gave both boys a treatment on the nebulizer machine, which vaporized the asthma medicine and forced it deep into the boys' lungs. The boys didn't mind the nebulizer treatment because to receive it, they "smoked" on a plastic pipe. When we went back to the U.S. for our first home leave, we purchased a nebulizer of our own so we wouldn't have any more frantic calls to the doctor or late-evening races to the Health Unit.

Our scariest encounter with the boys' asthma occurred on a Pakistan International Airline (PIA) flight from Islamabad to Beijing. PIA had recently inaugurated this flight and because it was part of the flight plan from Islamabad to Tokyo, there was just a short stay on the tarmac in Beijing. I was alone with the boys and headed back to the U.S. for home leave, while Tim stayed behind in Islamabad because he hadn't built up enough leave time to join us.

Our flight took place in the early 1990s when smoking was still permitted on international flights. Our section of the plane was separated from the smoking section by only a thin blue curtain, and every time a passenger or stewardess went between sections of the plane, a veil of cigarette smoke wafted over our heads.

Scott was around eight or nine years old, and he started wheezing and having difficulties breathing. I alerted the flight staff of the problem and asked about oxygen, which I assumed would be on board the plane. There was none. I was frightened watching Scott struggle for his next breath.

The flight attendant indicated that when we landed in Beijing, they would have the airport doctor come on board and attend to Scott. We were moved to the first class cabin to be farther away from the smoke. Although we had gotten visas to transit Beijing, we weren't allowed to deplane in Beijing – merely be on the tarmac for the hour it took to refuel for our onward four-hour flight to Tokyo.

Finally we landed in Beijing, and the minutes ticked by as we waited for the doctor to come on board. Fifteen minutes, 20, 25, and then we were told that the airport doctor was nowhere to be found. The flight attendant said the airport would have to find a local doctor.

I was determined to raise a ruckus and play the diplomatic card in an effort to get Scott off the plane before we took off for Tokyo. By this time Scott's cheeks had lost their color as he struggled to draw air into his chest. He was depending on me, and I was willing to create an international incident in order to prevent the plane from taxiing away from its berth. I felt the fury of a mother bear protecting her young.

As we waited and I fretted and prayed while Scott wheezed and took puffs on his inhaler to no relief, we received looks of condolences from passengers seated nearby. There was nothing they could do.

More minutes ticked by, and by now we had been on the tarmac for 45 minutes. Still there was no airport doctor. Finally with ten minutes before wheels up, a young woman came on board to see Scott. Between her broken English and her skills as a doctor and my rudimentary Chinese, she was able to give Scott some medicine, which helped to open his airways. The plane took off for Tokyo, which we knew had a 24-hour airport clinic.

As soon as the plane lifted off, one of the male flight attendants sat down in a seat three rows behind us and promptly lit a cigarette. My nose started prickling at the smell of smoke, and I got up from my seat and indignantly asked him what he was doing. Hadn't he just witnessed my son suffering from an asthma attack because of cigarette smoke? He promptly put his cigarette out and apologized. I couldn't believe the stupidity of people – a flight attendant at that.

In Tokyo we saw the doctor, where Scott received a nebulizer treatment. We also arranged for a bottle of oxygen for our onward flight to Seattle, but it wasn't needed, and we arrived in Seattle without further incident.

After arriving back home in Salem, we visited a painter's supply shop and bought a painter's mask of bright blue rubber with two round white disks on either side of the nose piece. These contained the filters, which were supposed to filter out most airborne pollutants. On the return flights to Islamabad, Scott wore the mask, which made him look like a mosquito with large bug eyes. He delighted in using his finger as a proboscis and poking people while making buzzing sounds in the high-pitched drone of a pesky mosquito. Oh, the adaptability of young children...

During our four years in Pakistan, we experienced a climate that was very different from the one we were used to back home. The heat and humidity in April, May, and into June built to a crescendo until it was broken by the arrival of the monsoon rains. To make matters worse, the brain-fever bird's call would escalate octave by octave, higher and higher, saying "It's hot! It's hot!" as if we didn't know it already. The highest temperature I can remember from our time in Islamabad was 120 degrees. When it got that hot and I had to park the car in the parking lot at work, the horn would short out and keep honking when I turned right.

There were other oddities to living in Islamabad. Driving was extremely unpredictable, and you would never know when you would encounter a pile of rocks on the road, left by a driver who had repaired his car in the middle where it had broken down. Outside of town you would have to dodge herds of goats, ox carts pulled by humped-back oxen moving at a glacial pace, and a stray camel or two.

In town, I said a prayer whenever I got behind the wheel because pedestrians would step out onto the road without looking, confident that Allah would protect them. He didn't always. The Regional Security Office warned us about being involved in a car accident, and if we were, we would need to drive away quickly and immediately contact the U.S. Embassy via radio, for vigilantism would take over and crowds of men and boys would soon form to avenge the death or injury of one of their own. It would be assumed that the "rich" American was at fault. High-tailing it from the scene of an accident ran counter to everything we learned in the U.S., but fortunately, we never had to run from an angry crowd.

In general, there was a lack of knowledge among the local population about food hygiene and safety. I was horrified to see bright green, blue, and pink pellets baked into bread that was sold at the bakery, the Kaka House in Supermarket. The name says it all. According to the rumors, the flour millers were having problems with rodents eating their flour, so they mixed pesticides directly into it. It was also in Islamabad that Brian started to cry while eating his morning cereal. We had bought the Pakistani version of Kix, and when he chewed, a sliver of steel had gotten embedded between his two front teeth. We stopped buying processed food on the local market and shopped at the Commissary for those items, instead.

We were delighted to find a large number of used bookstores in Islamabad that sold books in English, thanks to the history of British rule in the sub-continent. It was a treat for all of us to visit the bookstores, where we bought new books and re-sold ones we had already read. Our sons, Brian and Scott, developed wonderful reading skills, in part because of the plethora of bookstores but also because we didn't have local TV. There were local TV stations, but since none of us spoke Urdu, it didn't make for easy viewing.

The American Club on the Embassy grounds became our hangout on the weekends because it was a place we could go to and just be ourselves, without being stared at. The Embassy had a swimming pool, a restaurant and snack bar, a movie theater, where they showed family movies on Friday nights, several ball fields, and a compound where we could walk away from prying eyes. It was the perfect place to meet friends and just hang out.

A State Department psychiatrist came to the Embassy to talk to parents about Third Culture Kids and how to help them adjust to living in a foreign country. His advice was to give our children large doses of Americana in order to give them a strong identity of who they were. We enrolled our boys in Cub Scouts, and Tim and the other fathers took the boys on campouts and helped them work on their badges. We decorated our artificial Christmas tree and listened to Christmas carols while baking cookies together. We celebrated Thanksgiving with a traditional turkey dinner and all the trimmings.

Since this was our first post, I didn't have any other experiences to use as a filter through which to view Pakistan's interpretation of Islam. My subsequent experiences living in the more moderate Islamic countries of Egypt, Bangladesh, and Indonesia convinced me that I liked other countries' interpretation of Islam better. Pakistan would lie near the extreme end of the Islamic fundamentalism spectrum, but it wouldn't occupy the very end. That pride of place would belong to Saudi Arabia or Afghanistan. Still, the thousands of young boys who were schooled in

Islamist madrassas meant that there were ever-growing numbers of men who were inclined to believe in the Wahabi views of Islam that originated in Saudi Arabia more so than the more liberal westward-leaning views of Islam promulgated by western-educated Pakistanis. These western-educated people were for the most part, the silent minority.

As a family we attended the Protestant International Church, and it was our first exposure to worshiping with families from many countries and many denominations. We first met in a house near the Covered Market. Because of the diversity within our congregation, we had to boil our beliefs down to the basics: a dependence on the Bible as the written word of God and a belief in Jesus Christ as our personal Savior. There was no quibbling about sprinkling versus immersion in baptism nor about the choice of hymns to sing. Our church functioned much as we imagined the early Christian churches in Paul's day did. Long-time missionary families that had served in Pakistan for several generations were well represented, and we had Quakers, Baptists, Nazarenes, Methodists, Presbyterians, Assembly of God, and all other manner of Protestants. If you were Catholic, you attended the Catholic Church in Islamabad. Our church was directed by the government to minister to the needs of expats, so there were very few Pakistanis in our congregation. Evangelizing Muslims was against the law, and we knew that there were watchers in the congregation, those who worked for the Pakistani government and were paid to keep an eye on the goings-on in church.

It was outside the church one Friday morning (Friday was the day for worship) where we added to our family. Standing outside the entrance to the church was an expat holding a box of kittens, and the kittens were ready for adoption. The boys pleaded with me, "Please, pretty please, Mom, can we get a kitten?" Tim and I had been thinking that the boys would benefit from the unconditional love a pet gives. We caved in after one look at the black and white kitten with liquid green eyes, and on the way home, the boys christened the ball of fur Curious George, for the kitten's curious nature and his clambering all over the back seat on the drive home.

George was a wonderful addition to the family, and he looked like a Holstein cow because of his markings. He was a tolerant cat and allowed Brian to sling him over his shoulder and carry him around the house. He also became an indoor/outdoor cat, and we would leave the study window open so that George could go outside to explore whenever he wanted to. This practice of allowing George to exit and reenter the study window at will ended when we moved to our new home on Margalla Avenue. In the new neighborhood, there was a big tomcat that would beat George up, and we feared one night he might not return, so we had to keep George inside from then on. Fortunately, we had an enclosed screened porch at the second house, and George could be found there most of the time sniffing the outside air.

George also had a disconcerting habit of sitting by the side of the floor drain in the evening, waiting for the cockroaches to come crawling out. We learned the intricacies of Pakistani plumbing, which called for a slanted cement slab under the enclosed tub, which allowed the water to drain directly into the ground underneath the house. There was a hole in the tiling near the floor to allow for overflow of the drain water. Unfortunately, this hole also allowed cockroaches to enter the bathroom, and George delighted in batting them around. Because of George's habit of tormenting the cockroaches, he often developed unexplained fevers and lethargy, and I would take him to the local vet, who would give George an antibiotic shot.

One of George's more endearing habits was to stand on Tim's lap with his forepaws on Tim's chest and nuzzle noses with Tim. We all came under George's spell and quickly became cat lovers.

Although I was never particularly squeamish when it came to bugs, I became less squeamish as time overseas wore on. Our second home had a larger backyard, so we were able to grow a vegetable garden where we planted carrots, tomatoes, broccoli, and cauliflower. I remember feeling so proud of our cauliflower, which had tight, white heads. The problem was that we had planted too many of them, and our family couldn't eat them all, so I gave some to our friends.

The problem occurred when I started blanching a few of the cauliflower heads before freezing them and found the surface of the water in the pot covered with little black dots. Apparently, the bugs had hidden themselves deep within the cauliflower, and the boiling water had forced them out. I sheepishly apologized to Cheryl the next time I saw her. She replied, "No problem. I just put more pepper on the cauliflower and the family never knew the difference." Cheryl was the mother of four, and this was their second overseas post, so she was quite laid-back about the whole thing.

Expats had to be pretty nonchalant about a lot of things overseas, and the following joke reflects the attitude we all eventually adopted as a way to preserve our sanity: At your first post when you spot a fly in your soup, you call the waiter over and have him give you a new bowl. At your second post when you see a fly in your soup, you merely fish the fly out and continue eating. At your third post when you order a bowl of soup and it arrives without a fly, you call the waiter over and ask him, "Waiter, where's my fly?"

Because we lived in a sub-tropical region, our houses came equipped with geckoes, which climbed the walls with their suction-cup feet and serenaded us with their chirps. The geckoes tormented George, and he would sit mesmerized waiting for one of them to creep within his reach. Ants were another bother, and we had to keep our kitchen meticulously clean and free of sugar spills. Mosquitoes were a problem for which we had to take malaria medicine. Mondays were malaria days, so we all had to force the bitter pill down our throats at breakfast time.

The thing I feared most when arriving in Pakistan never happened. We had read to the boys Rudyard Kipling's book, <u>Riki Tiki Tavi</u>, about a pet mongoose that saves a little boy from being bitten by a cobra. Cobras were native to Pakistan, but perhaps the most feared snake is the krait, whose bite is deadly. Our front door had a two-inch gap at the bottom, just enough room for a snake to enter. As soon as I could, I asked the General Services Office (GSO), which was responsible for household repairs in our leased houses, to put a door sweep on the bottom. Thankfully, we never saw any cobras or kraits except in a facility we toured near Rawalpindi, where they milked snakes for their venom. The older, white-bearded man who demonstrated how to milk a snake had lost one of his index fingers to a snake bite.

The oddities of living in Islamabad were offset by the serendipities we encountered, which included having a guava tree in our backyard and watching the long-tailed green parrots fly in formation overhead before settling in our tree. I learned that I didn't like guavas for their gritty taste, but I delighted in watching the showy birds chow down on the fruit.

§

The war in Afghanistan between the competing Mujahideen groups was brought home to us with the kidnapping of one of our church members, Joel, who was an interpreter for an American veterinarian who was vaccinating domestic animals in eastern Afghanistan. The veterinarian was released after three months due to his ill health, but Joel was held for six months and was moved from place to place, always in a remote area, to avoid being detected. At first, the kidnappers thought

Joel was Afghan because he wore a shalwar kurta, sported a long beard, and spoke fluent Dari. Joel had grown up in Pakistan in a missionary family and was as much at home in the Pakistani culture as he was in the American.

During this time, Mark, who was in charge of the vaccination project, kept working through official and non-official channels to get both Joel and the doctor released. Our church held prayer vigils and sought God's protection for their health and safety. As it turned out, Joel and the doctor had been kidnapped by one of the lesser warlord groups. The leaders of the group thought if they kidnapped a westerner, they could gain recognition for their group and become eligible to receive the arms and ammunition being divvied up among the seven major Mujahideen groups in Afghanistan. Arms were being funneled through ISI, the intelligence branch of the Pakistani Government. Six months after Joel's capture he was released to the joy and relief of his friends, family, and church. We held a welcome home celebration at church and commemorated the event with a decorated cake and much rejoicing.

Pakistan in the late 1980s and early 1990s was not immune from the geopolitical struggles taking place next door in Afghanistan because it also faced a growing conflict between the ideologies of Islamic fundamentalism and the more secular allure of the western world. It was not an easy balancing act, and relations between Pakistan and the U.S. were tenuous at best. As the tensions mounted in the lead-up to The Gulf War in early 1991, a decision was made to evacuate the official American community to safety back in the U.S. The following is an account of our evacuation and the turmoil we felt at that time.

It's a Small World

...Though the mountains divide,
And the oceans are wide,
It's a small world after all.

That was the song that we awoke to in the Disneyland Hotel on January 16, 1991, the day The Gulf War was declared. We had just been evacuated from Pakistan, and somehow the saccharin-sweet melody and lyrics did not compute with what we had experienced in the months leading up to the war and on our 36-hour flight from Pakistan.

Although the government of Pakistan officially supported the U.S. and its Allies in The Gulf War, most Pakistanis rallied behind Saddam Hussein. Tensions hovered in the orange zone, and I remember feeling like a potential target because I was American. I would drive a circuitous route to my friend Fran's house to avoid driving past the Iraqi Embassy. Fran decided to take a proactive approach to the Iraqis; she waved at the guards as she drove by, hoping that international politics would not be played out at the individual level.

Evacuation started with a surreptitious knock on the door by our USAID Deputy Executive Officer at 3 a.m. on January 14. He had been working around-the-clock trying to get all the tickets in order for the chartered flights out of Islamabad. The plane hopscotched from Islamabad to Karachi to Bangkok to Manila to Tokyo, and finally to Los Angeles, where we planned to overnight before my husband departed to Washington D.C. The boys and I planned to return to Salem, Oregon where our young sons had been enrolled in elementary school. Our strategy was to put the boys in a school they were familiar with. We needed a respite from too much reality, so we decided to spoil ourselves with some fantasy before being separated for six months.

I remember feeling a disconnect with the 24-hour news coverage from CNN about our enemies, the Iraqis, and the It's a Small World melody blasting from the loudspeakers advocating brotherly love. More than oceans divided the Allies from the Iraqis. Recent history suggests that a gulf still exists between them and us, but I'm hopeful that common sense can prevail to prevent yet another war in Iraq. As the lyrics go, "There's so much that we share, that it's time we're aware, it's a small world after all."[1]

§

The abrupt dislocation of our previous lives in Islamabad and the sudden relocation back to the States and separation of our family created its own stresses. From Los Angeles, our family split up with Tim continuing on to Washington, D.C. to return to work and the boys and I returning to Salem, Oregon, where we had lived prior to Tim's joining USAID. We knew that we would be separated for at least six months, so I settled into my role as both mom and dad to our two boys, now ages 9 and 10. The boys were at that active stage where they liked to

---

[1] First published in *The Foreign Service Journal March 2003*

roughhouse with their dad, and I felt Tim's absence immensely. Every boy needs his dad. As a mom, my personality lent itself to the business end of things – brushing teeth and taking baths; reading bedtime stories; doing homework; and making sure the boys ate their vegetables. I liked cuddling but not getting down on all fours to give horsey back rides.

This was also my first time living on my own and being responsible for two small children because I had gone from my parents' home to the home Tim and I shared when I got married at the age of 19. All of a sudden I was responsible for doing all those things I had relied on Tim for previously. I had much need of prayer, and I sought the Lord's guidance on a daily basis. At our church there was an old wooden yoke hanging above the sanctuary entrance. Next to the yoke was the verse, "Take my yoke upon you and learn from me, for I am gentle and humble in heart, and you will find rest for your souls. For my yoke is easy and my burden is light." (Matthew 11:29-30 NIV)

While in Salem, I discovered the joys of church community once again because the church became our extended family and provided for most of our physical, spiritual, and emotional needs. The church members equipped our apartment with all the necessities in the interim period before the travel ban was lifted and we could return to Islamabad and join Tim. The pastor and his wife even lent us their second car, which was dubbed "The White Whale" for my once a week 50-mile commute to Portland to meet my advisor while I worked on my thesis for my Master's degree in Teaching English as a Second Language. I had previously completed all the coursework for the degree at Portland State University but had not been able to complete the thesis before we were sent to Pakistan with USAID. It was now or never, so I settled into a routine of walking the boys to school in the morning and returning to our apartment each day to concentrate on writing. Day by day, week by week, month by month my thesis took form, and I was able to complete it and defend it before my panel of advisors by the time Tim returned from overseas to accompany us back to Islamabad, where we completed our final two years.

After returning, I took a job as the TOEFL Coordinator for the Academy for Educational Development. I administered the TOEFL (test of English as a foreign language) to Pakistani examinees who were going to the U.S. for either an undergraduate or a graduate degree. This job allowed me to travel to the regional capitals of Pakistan, and I was able to see a wide swathe of the country. We travelled as a team of three, and I discovered that each of the regional cities had a different vibe and character. Peshawar was the Wild West of Pakistan, and it was not unusual to see men carrying their Kalashnikovs or Lee Enfield rifles through town with a bandolier of bullets strapped across their chests. Their turbans, beards, and fierce looks helped to contribute to their wild and wooly unfettered tribal image. The Intercontinental Hotel in Peshawar had a sign prominently displayed in the lobby: All guests must check their guns at the front desk.

Quetta in Baluchistan felt very tribal and it was the place to look for tribal rugs. Karachi was a congested seaport with a mix of Punjabis, Sindhis, Baluchis, Pathans, and every tribal affiliation you can imagine. Lahore was considered the cultural capital of Pakistan because of the splendor of its monuments dating back to the Mughal period. Lahore was also the only city where I encountered one examinee who received a perfect score on the TOEFL.

While administering the TOEFL in the various cities, I had to contend with issues that testers in more developed regions never encountered. In Peshawar, I had to stop the recording of the listening portion of the test to allow for the roar of the F–16s to diminish as they passed overhead. In Lahore, I had to wait while a female examinee lifted her burkha so that I could ascertain her identity from her identity card. In Quetta during the winter, examinees often appeared for the test dressed in warm sweaters, coats, and gloves because the cavernous testing center lacked an adequate heating system. I carried extra batteries for the boom box because I would never know when the power would go out and the recording for the listening portion stop. Because many of the test examinees had never been out of the country and had not been exposed to western females, we were encouraged to wear western dress during the administration of the test.

I felt privileged to be able to see so much of the country, and as a team, we always tried to take advantage of a few hours to explore the markets such as the Qissa Khawani or Bazaar of the Storytellers in Peshawar. It was there that I bought dried figs strung on a rope. They had been flattened and a hole pierced through the center in order to be strung. In Karachi we explored Saddar Bazaar, the main shopping area filled with narrow alleyways with rows and rows of clothing. It was in this market that I bought Tim a marine compass salvaged from a cargo ship that had been driven up on the sand to be plucked for parts much like a chicken carcass is plucked of its meat after cooking. Karachi had a large shipwrecking industry, and the markets bulged with brass and copper fittings from ships: captain's wheels, compasses, towel bars, and door knockers. Quetta was a great place to buy tribal rugs, and we spent many an hour sipping tea with the proprietors of the rug shops viewing their treasures from Baluchistan or Afghanistan, many of which sported pictures of tanks and arms so reminiscent of the war.

I reveled in exploring the arts and crafts in Pakistan, and we spent many Friday afternoons wandering through Juma (Friday) Bazaar in Islamabad, where Pakistani and Afghan merchants displayed their wares. Beads and tribal jewelry were big items as well as the flat-weave rugs called dhurries, and we bought several of them to cover the marble floors in our home. They were tightly woven and virtually indestructible for families with kids or pets. We couldn't yet afford to buy the Oriental rugs that were so coveted, so for the first three years of our posting we contented ourselves with the dhurries.

One of my favorite Afghan merchants at Juma Bazaar had sandy hair and blue eyes, and I always perused his jewelry closely. I wondered how he had acquired his light coloring and if he was one of Alexander the Great's descendants, for the story is that Alexander the Great left some of his men behind when he departed the area. His men intermarried with the local women, producing children with blue or green eye color.

One of my goals before leaving Pakistan was to buy a large Oriental carpet, but since we didn't know anything about carpets, we decided to hold off on what we assumed to be a large purchase. In preparation for buying carpets, we attended classes that one of our colleagues, Al, taught at the Asian Study Group. He had been a Peace Corps volunteer in Iran years earlier and as a way to combat boredom in his little town, he hung around carpet shops and acquired a wealth of knowledge about local weavings, which he shared with the expat population in Islamabad.

At a cocktail party, Al asked me what type of carpet I liked. I replied that I'd like an 8' x 10' double-knotted carpet in perhaps pinks and blues, but I didn't really like the tribal designs that were so prevalent in the markets. Al said he'd keep that in mind. Two months later, I received a call from Al saying that a man from Lahore would drop a carpet off at our house, and he would return a month later to see if we wanted to buy it. Sure enough, an hour later a man with a roll of carpet sticking out the window of his Volkswagon bug knocked at the door. He rolled the carpet out on our living room floor and explained that you had to live with a carpet in order to decide whether the carpet was meant for you. He also said that this particular carpet was a twin to the one Nawaz Sharif, the former Prime Minister of Pakistan, had in his home.

We didn't know if we believed the Nawaz Sharif story, but we decided to look at carpet shops in earnest to figure out what we really wanted. We had a month before the man would return. The more we visited the local shops, the more we realized that the carpet we liked was already sitting in our living room. The carpet man returned in a month, and we negotiated a price, but we told him we couldn't really afford such a large investment. He replied that it was no problem – he would take monthly payments, and we paid off the carpet in a little more than a year. Twenty years later the carpet occupies a prominent place in our bedroom and our hearts.

We were fortunate to live in Pakistan during a time that was not as volatile as later years. Despite the fact that the Russians had recently pulled out of Afghanistan and Pakistan was reeling from an influx of several million refugees, the country was still relatively stable. We were able to travel throughout the northern areas and see sights few tourists have seen.

Tim and a friend, Jesse, traveled to Chitral and Swat in the Northern Territory and rafted the Indus and Kunar rivers with Walgis Travel, a local travel agency, in their inaugural rafting tour of Pakistan's northern rivers. Walgis had employed the great-great grandson of the famous Speakes who along with his partner, Burton, had discovered the headwaters of the Nile. Michael spent six months of the year with Walgis, training river guides for the waters of Pakistan and the remaining six months rafting an array of rivers around the world, including the Zambezi River in Africa. A video tape made of that inaugural trip called "Rafting the Kunar" still resides in the video library of the Foreign Service Institute in Arlington, Virginia. It features Tim and four other Americans on their rafting adventure.

It was on one of Tim and Jesse's rafting expeditions up north that they *did* discover the mythical Spanish-speaking community Tim had dreamed of. In one of the tiny towns in the Northern Areas, their four-wheel drive vehicle broke down. They found a mechanic's shop, but the Americans couldn't communicate with the Pakistani mechanic. Jesse, who had lived in the Asian subcontinent for years, tried Urdu, Nepali, and Bangla, all to no effect. It wasn't until another rafting partner, Dave, started swearing in Spanish that the mechanic's ears perked up. As it turned out, the Pakistani mechanic had worked as a taxi driver in Spain, and he spoke Spanish. Between Dave's and the mechanic's Spanish, their vehicle was repaired.

We took another memorable trip to the Khunjerab Pass between China and Pakistan. The route took us along the Karakoram Highway, the historic road that followed the traditional Silk Road, which was a feat of engineering and cooperation between Pakistan and China. It had been built at the cost of hundreds of lives. It traversed the Karakoram mountain range, known to have the highest concentration of peaks over 8,000m in the world. We saw evidence of the meaning of Karakoram, a Turkic word for black gravel, in every turn of the road, and we hoped that the loose gravel and massive boulders would not threaten our trip with landslides. We felt privileged to be traveling in the footsteps of Alexander the Great and Genghis Khan, and the passes through which we traveled were as much steeped in history as the tea in the cups of chai (milky tea spiced with cardamom) we consumed.

Two other expat families traveled with us – one Canadian family and another American, both of whom worked in development. Among us we had four boys between the ages of nine and ten. The plan was to fly into Gilgit, in the Northern Areas and rent a van to start our trip. Because Gilgit is situated at 5,000 feet elevation at the base of a bowl of mountains in the Rakaposhi Range, the Fokker Friendship planes needed to fly in a tight corkscrew pattern, skirting around Nanga Parbat, nicknamed "Killer Mountain," to descend to the airport. We knew that statistically, only 25% of the planes bound for Gilgit ever made a landing. The remaining 75% had to be turned back to the originating airport due to inclement weather. The pilot of the plane invited passengers to view the panorama of mountains which were arrayed before us as far as the eye could see. The view from the cockpit was stunning. Fate was shining on us, and we were able to land in Gilgit, where we overnighted at the Serena Hotel and watched as the setting sun burnished the mountains with pink and orange brushstrokes. We departed for the border between Pakistan and China the next morning.

We rented a van with two drivers, one of whom rode shotgun as a mechanic and alternate driver. By the time we were two hours out of Gilgit, we were being driven crazy by the boys' bathroom jokes and the never-ending question of "Are we there yet?", questions and jokes that nine and ten-year-old boys do best. We decided to scrap the plan of driving to the Khunjerab Pass to China and instead, do whatever was needed to make the boys happy. We figured that if the boys were happy, the parents would be happy.

Jesse, who'd had experience in Outward Bound in the U.S., had thought ahead and had brought along rock hammers for the boys. We also came armed with Isobel Shaw's <u>Pakistan Handbook</u>, which told us which road marker to stop at to find veins of garnets and rubies in the cliff faces. Apparently by the time we had discovered the guidebook, others had as well, so the veins of gems were depleted, but the boys had a blast clambering over the rocks and pounding on them.

We reached Hunza, where we visited Altit and Baltit forts, mountain strongholds in Hunza which guarded feudal kingdoms from centuries past. Each fort was perched on a mountain top and separated from the other by the Hunza River far below. We heard Machiavellian stories of how the kings in times past had thrown their enemies over the cliff side to fall to their deaths on the rocks. Baltit Fort, which dates from the 16th century, shows Tibetan influences in its carving, when a Baltit princess imported a master carver to renovate the fort as part of her dowry. The people speak Wakhi, a language similar to what is spoken in the Wakhan Corridor, the sliver of land in Afghanistan that separates Pakistan from China.

We decided to journey only as far as Gulmit, a village at the base of the Passu Cones, a range of saw-toothed mountains that formed part of the Karakoram Range. We stopped for the night at the Marco Polo Inn, which was open for one more week before it closed for the season. The gateway to the inn was mounted with large Marco Polo sheep horns, and we entered to find our rooms at the inn, featuring thick, quilted comforters from China, lace curtains on the windows, and a flower vase with a plastic flower. The weather was frosty cold, even in early October, so we bundled up in our wool sweaters and thick down jackets. Dinner that evening was eaten around a kerosene lamp (they had power for only a few hours a day due to load shedding) and featured a chicken curry with rice, dhal and chapattis, a delicious spinach dish, and lots of chai.

Some people claim that Hunza is the fabled Shangri-La, where people subsist on apricots and live to 100 years of age. In Gulmit we also visited the motel owner's small dusty museum showcasing artifacts from his ancestors. There were gems mined from the local area, old cooking utensils, and even a stuffed snow leopard. The motel owner had inherited the title of Mir of Hunza, although he no longer fought pitched battles with other kings of the mountainous region.

On the return trip, the Gilgit valley was socked in with low-lying clouds, so returning by plane to Islamabad was out of the question, and we had to rent a van and driver for our 17-hour drive back. We got two drivers, and we soon learned that the second driver's job was to keep the main driver awake. The road hugged the side of the mountain and presented us with awe-inspiring views of the river 1,000 feet below. One friend, Dick, had a fear of heights and was ashen faced for most of the trip as he averted his eyes from the vertiginous cliffs and the roiling river far below. We all hoped that our van would not be found lying at the bottom of the ravine after having "turned turtle" as the Pakistanis are fond of saying.

We discovered that the second driver's job included paying baksheesh whenever we were stopped by local highwaymen extorting money from travelers. We finally made it back to Islamabad 17 body-and-mind- numbing hours later, happy to be home. Our guidebook by the indefatigable Isobel Shaw remains in our bookshelf, but since it was well loved and its pages well thumbed, the cover has torn away from the binding, exposing the spine. The yellowed sections remain a testament to our adventures and travels throughout Pakistan.

§

Brian and Scott attended the International School of Islamabad (ISI), located on the outskirts of the city. The school employed American and Pakistani staff and was run on an American school system. It was an excellent school attended by children from all around the world. Much of the expat community's social life revolved around the school's activities, and it was here where the boys were introduced to drama.

Both boys took music lessons as part of their school curricula, and their music teacher recruited them as workhouse boys for the musical, *Oliver*. The music teacher was part of the local amateur theatrical group, Rawalpindi Amateur Theatrical Society (RATS). The rehearsal schedule was quite daunting for a seven-year-old, and Scott came home one day from the daily rehearsals exhausted and in tears. He wanted to quit. Tim and I saw this situation as a wonderful learning opportunity, so we told Scott that since he had committed to his music teacher and the play, he would have to tell his teacher he wanted to quit, not us. After pondering the situation, Scott decided that the rehearsal schedule was less daunting than dealing with his teacher, so Scott continued in the play. We were proud of both of our sons.

In the third grade Scott had a teacher named Mrs. Sandquist; she was beloved for her teaching skills as well as her penchant for everything related to turtles, and everyone knew her as the turtle teacher. The following article is one that I wrote about one of my favorite keepsakes and the memories it recalls.

The Watch

One of my most prized possessions is a gold-colored watch in the shape of a serpent. It curls around my wrist and has a watch face encased by a serpent's head, encircled with tiny crystals intended to represent real diamonds. There is one missing crystal, but it's not noticeable unless you inspect the watch carefully. The body of the serpent is segmented and has gold-colored "skin" etched in a diamond reptilian design.

The watch no longer runs, and the metal on the inside of the band is corroded and starting to rust due to much wearing in the heat and humidity of Pakistan. Never mind. The watch's value comes not from its design, its ability to keep time, or the value of the materials it contains. Its value is sentimental because it was bought at a great price: 143 turtles in fact.

Scott's third-grade teacher had a classroom which reflected her love of turtles. She motivated her students by giving them paper turtles for a job well done: reading x number of pages in a story, turning in a writing assignment on time, exemplary behavior in class, or math homework done correctly. At the end of the year and for special holidays, the students could redeem their turtles, which were tabulated, and the children could buy gifts at the class store with their turtles. Mrs. Sandquist bought trinkets and small gifts at the variety stores in town to stock her turtle store, and the children eagerly anticipated the gifts they could purchase with their turtles.

The students were studying idioms as part of their language curriculum, and their teacher challenged them to write down as many idioms as they could to bring to class the next day. Little did Mrs. Sandquist know that Scott's mother, an ESL teacher, was the idiom queen.

Scott came home from school that day, and we sat down at the dining room table to puzzle out as many idioms as we could. The list soon flowed: It's raining cats and dogs; knee-high to a grasshopper; the straw that broke the camel's back; she's the spitting image of her mother, and on and on until both Scott and I had exhausted our brains and our fingers for a grand total of 143 idioms.

True to her word, the next day Mrs. Sandquist shelled out 143 paper turtles, which Scott used to buy the serpent watch. I remember the pride on Scott's freckled face as he presented the Mother's Day gift he had chosen for me. I cherish the watch as a symbol of Scott's hard work and his selflessness in choosing the perfect gift for me, one which was paid for at a high price – 143 turtles.

§

Because my job as TOEFL Coordinator was intermittent, I was able to take on a second job as a member of the Roster, a list of spouses who performed tasks for USAID on a short-term contract basis. Throughout the three years I remained on the Roster, I had a variety of jobs: creating a library of procurement materials for the Procurement Office; editing a housing project survey; editing two socioeconomic profiles for the Northwest Frontier Province; warehousing and distributing a half million forms for a Child Survival Project; and creating a scrapbook for the environmental docudrama, "Before It's Too Late."

This last job was my favorite job because it allowed me to travel to Lahore and work with the director of the film, Shireen Pasha. My job was to document the still shots for the film, describing and putting them in a scrapbook to capture the making of the film. The film showed the environmental degradation of Pakistan through the eyes of an elderly patriarch. Since the literacy rate in Pakistan was low and because Pakistan had traditionally been an oral society, the American producer of the film, Ron, thought that a docudrama was the best way to educate the Pakistani populace about the dangers of water and air pollution, soil erosion, and the depletion of forests and fishing areas. The urgency of the environmental degradation suggested the title of the film – "Before It's Too Late." The film was shown throughout Pakistan and even shown at the 1992 environmental conference in Rio de Janeiro. I was proud to be part of the film team, even though I had a minute role in it.

Another memorable experience occurred on my last TOEFL testing trip to Quetta. It was spring that March day in 1993 in Baluchistan. The apple trees were just starting to send forth their white blossoms, some like popped popcorn on the branches, others like hard kernels, waiting for the signal to open.

The air was cool and full of promise as we drove eastward toward the Bolan Pass, that historic southern gateway through the Toba Kakar Range of mountains to the Baluch interior. My boss, Lance, and I had rented a yellow taxi and driver to take us to Sibi to see the horse and camel market, where traders from all over Pakistan came to trade their animals.

Our taxi rattled and bucked its way down the road, and each bump made me wince as I tried to keep my neck and head relaxed and upright, my cervical collar a shock absorber to elongate my vertebrae. Weeks earlier I had been sledding with my husband and sons in Murree, a hill station northeast of Rawalpindi, and although I had successfully negotiated the snowy slope twice on the flying saucer, the third attempt sent me head over teakettle to land on my head. I heard a sickening crack before struggling to sit upright, and I hoped I had not done any permanent damage. I learned later that I had damaged the cartilage in my upper back and not the vertebrae, thankfully. For the next several weeks I wore the cervical collar, and like the thick woolen sock my mom made me wear around my neck as a child when I had a chest cold, the collar collected heat and caused my skin to chafe.

My view of the rocky terrain outside the taxi window was interrupted occasionally by a glimpse of the black felt tents of the Kochi nomads, who made camp on their journey north to seek greener pastures for their herds of sheep, goats, and camels.

We stopped along the side of the road to photograph the caravan plodding by and saw a black-clad, veiled woman atop one of the larger camels. She turned her head away as we took her picture. Her cargo was a bundle of sticks and a white fabric bag, perhaps holding all her worldly possessions. Her camel was trailed by a baby camel, a month old, a third of its mother's height, and it walked on improbably spindly legs.

The tires thrummed as we crossed the concrete bridges with livestock guards on either end. Off in the distance we spied a shepherd guiding his flock of wooly sheep and goats toward the stream down below the road. Was he also taking his flock to Sibi?

What a perfect picture opportunity! Lance and I instructed our driver to depart from the macadam road and onto the winding track of dirt and gravel that led down the slope to the stream, where the shepherd and his animals were lingering.

Lance and I approached the white-turbaned shepherd, and Lance started talking with him in Urdu. Since I couldn't speak more than just the basics of the language, I hung back and focused on the newborn goat kids that nestled in the fabric panniers that hung on each side of the donkey. The kids were just a day old and were getting a free ride, unlike the other members of their flock. Curiously, I had never before noticed the narrow strip of chocolate-colored fur that ran the length of the donkey's spine. That line was bisected by a shorter perpendicular line just behind the donkey's shoulder blades, giving the effect of a cross.

Suddenly, our idyllic rural scene was interrupted by the arrival of a Toyota Hilux pickup that came barreling down the gravel road, its bed filled with Kalashnikov-toting gunmen, their heads topped with black turbans. We heard them before we saw them.

It was then I remembered that both Lance and I had forgotten the cardinal rule in the Tribal Areas: the Pakistani government's jurisdiction and protection apply only when you are on the main roads in the Tribal Areas, and when you stray from the road you are subject to tribal law.

A man who I assumed to be the one in charge jumped out of the cab of the truck and strode toward Lance and the taxi driver while shouting at both of them. I was standing perhaps 30 feet from Lance, having wandered down to the stream to dip my toes in the water. Now as I listened to the angry altercation between the headman, Lance, and our driver, I tried to make myself as inconspicuous as a woman in that situation could be. There were 8-10 gunmen at the ready, their hands clutching their guns in an imperious manner. As I focused on the gunmen, fears of gang rape and even murder entered my consciousness. Images of newspaper headlines flashed before my eyes: Authorities Search for Two Americans Kidnapped in Baluchistan. It hadn't been that long since one of our church members had been kidnapped by a minor Mujahideen group in Afghanistan, and his six-month ordeal was fresh in my mind.

Although I couldn't understand Lance's Urdu, I could see that he was pleading mea culpa for ignoring tribal law. Our taxi driver seemed to be doing the same. I kept backing up, trying to put as much distance between me and the men as possible, although I knew it wouldn't do much good. The stream was narrow, the bed rocky, and I was the lone western woman facing a tribal warlord and his armed henchmen.

Upon orders by the warlord, one of his men started hitting our driver about the head and raining blows on his body. Lance's voice escalated as he apologized for our infraction. After what seemed like an eternity, the warlord told his man to stop; perhaps he was satisfied he had made his point. We were told that we were free to go, and the warlord got back into the truck, which sped away, spraying a cloud of dirt and gravel from the rear tires.

It must have been 30 seconds or so before the three of us realized our good fortune to have escaped the wrath of the tribal warlord with a minimum of damage. Our driver wiped his bloody nose and walked gingerly back to the taxi with Lance and I following close behind.

Collectively, we breathed a sigh of relief after the taxi engine sputtered to life, and we pulled off the dirt track onto the main road heading toward Quetta. All thoughts about seeing Sibi were forgotten as we apologized to our driver over and over again for having gotten him into that mess. I dug into my purse for Tylenol and Band-Aids to staunch the cuts he had sustained on his head. He had suffered for our rash decision to stray from the road, all for the sake of the pictures we took.

The drive back to Quetta was a sober one as we reconstructed the scene, both Lance and I lamenting our stupidity in the fiasco. Had our status as Americans saved us from more severe consequences? Maybe, but I also credit the guardian angel who was protecting us that day.

Chapter Two • Egypt

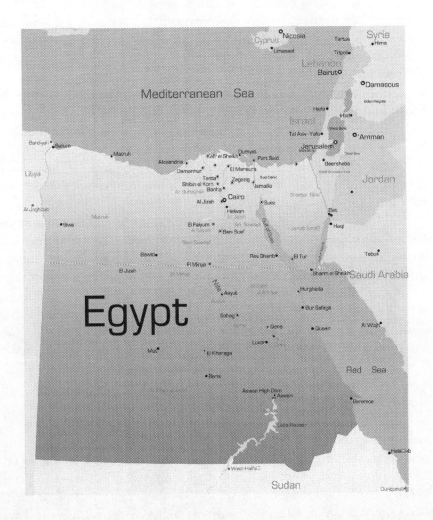

O God, help me to follow you wherever you may lead me... Our next post was Cairo, Egypt, where we lived from 1993 to 1997. Cairo was our family's favorite post for a number of reasons. Egyptians, who were known as the clowns of the Arab world, were forever making fun of themselves with obvious good humor. They had a laissez-faire outlook on life, probably acquired after centuries of exposure to other cultures. Egypt was also at the crossroads of many important civilizations throughout history, and their hieroglyphs testified to the invasions of every ancient potentate in the Middle East and some who were not – Napoleon Bonaparte, for example.

The city was called Mother of the World by the Arabs, and we found the Egyptians to be warm, friendly, and not xenophobic. Their interpretation of Islam was not as fundamentalist as that of Pakistan, and there was a sizeable Christian Coptic population, representing 10% of the total population. Because of Egypt's central location in the Middle East, we were able to travel to Israel to see the Holy Land, to Kenya to experience a photo safari, to the Sinai desert to walk in the footsteps of Moses and the Israelites, and to the Western Desert, where Alexander the Great traversed the desert sands. We went on two Nile cruises and took in as much ancient history of the pharaohs as our brains could absorb.

We lived in Ma'adi, a suburb 20-30 minutes south of the city center, where the Embassy and the USAID office were located near Tahrir Square. In Cairo as in Islamabad, I took the first year off from work to focus on settling the family in our new post. I also took Arabic classes through the Community Services Association (CSA) with the goal of learning enough Arabic to communicate the basics with Egyptians. After a year of twice weekly Arabic lessons, I spoke Taxi Arabic – enough to get myself from point A to point B. Arabic was a difficult language and much different from the French, Bahasa Malaysia, and Mandarin Chinese languages I had studied previously. I found it difficult to understand the logic of Arabic, and I thought I'd never have enough spit to pronounce the guttural sounds that are so prevalent in that Semitic language.

We lived in a four-floor apartment building leased by the U.S. Government, called 11/11 for its address – house 11 on 11th street. We bid on this building because it had a basketball hoop in the central courtyard, and our son, Scott, was an avid basketball player. I still remember the phrase I used with taxi drivers to return home to our apartment in Ma'adi: "Ana ayza aruh shariah hidasher hidasher minfadlak" (I want to go to 11/11 please.) My ability to speak a little of the language came in handy when shopping in the Khan el Khalili, the famous bazaar which dates from the 1500s, and later in teaching English to my beginner's class of drivers and janitors at the Embassy.

Although I taught English at all levels from the pre-literate to advanced classes, my job teaching English to the drivers and janitors, some of whom were not literate in Arabic, was probably the most rewarding. I learned another Arabic phrase, which came in handy: "Il haruuf lazim takuun a'a la issatr." (The letters must sit on the line.) The beginning class had difficulty learning which letters of the English alphabet had a tail draped below the line and which sat on the line. They also had a letter in Arabic, the "ye," that looked like a lazy "s," which half-reclined on the line. These drivers and janitors, who were on the low end of the social spectrum of Egyptian society, were so appreciative of being given the opportunity to learn that they hung on my every word. We started with the letters of the alphabet and their sound/letter correspondence. By the time the class finished, the students could read and write simple phrases and communicate with Americans they interacted with in their jobs. These classes focused on work-related English and the vocabulary and phrases that would help improve the men's work skills.

One of our favorite pastimes was exploring the Khan el Khalili, and we would often go by taxi to the ancient market for a day of poking around. It was a chance to explore the rabbit warren of alleyways and to try our hand at bargaining for Egyptian handicrafts: brass lamps that emitted pinpricks of light through their latticework onion-dome tops; soutache-embroidered vests of watered silk, Egyptian figurines modeled from the mud of the Nile River; blown-glass Christmas ornaments in bird and camel shapes; silver charms in all shapes and sizes stamped 92.5 for the purity of their silver; butter-soft leather jackets; and precious and semi-precious stones from all over the world.

We learned early on to use our Arabic to converse with the proprietors of the shops and to shoot the breeze over a cup of steaming hot tea. A certain amount of phatic communication had to be used before getting down to the business of bargaining. How was business that day? How was the family? Did he have any children? We were tempted to buy the t-shirts many foreign residents sported that said, "We're residents, not tourists," so we could obtain the resident prices, but we didn't. We hoped our faltering language skills were enough to convince the merchants that we were not tourists. We also learned not to inquire about someone's wife because it was inappropriate to talk about female family members. The euphemism used for a wife is the word, house. At work it's common to hear someone convey a message by saying, "The house called this morning."

For lunch we would stop in the café that Naguib Mafouz, the Nobel Prize winning author of Midaq Alley, made famous and order the meze, a Turkish word for the combination of Mediterranean dishes of eggplant, stuffed grape leaves, and hummus with pita bread. Egyptian coffee was served in clear glasses with a thick residue of coffee at the bottom. Tim always confounded the café owner when he requested extra hot water to make the coffee last for two or three cups. Most cafes were redolent of incense and sights of patrons reclining on cushions, happily puffing on hookah pipes after a satisfying meal. Tea was served piping hot in a clear glass with fresh mint leaves on top, and you held the glass by fingertip until it cooled down.

The following article recounts our adventures exploring the Khan el Khalili, the ancient caravanserais of the old city, and the Street of the Tentmakers.

Faces of Egypt

"You dropped it." I looked down at the grime of the street, seemingly centuries old, expecting to see something I had dropped...a wallet, an address book. I looked up into the smiling eyes of the street vendor, his hands over his chest. He said with a bow, "You dropped it... my heart."

I offered up a smile and then hurried on. I was trying to keep up with friends who were already a hundred feet ahead of me in the throngs of people. I enjoyed poking around the bazaars and backstreets of Cairo and was looking forward to our evening plans to experience more of the "real" Egypt and to watch the whirling dervishes perform.

I joined the others as they moved toward the overpass. We ducked as a man riding a bicycle and balancing a huge basket of baladi (flat country) bread on his head wove his way through the crowd. He tsk-tsked as he pedaled, a non-verbal sign in Egypt that means "Coming through!"

We scooted around the old galabiyya-clad woman who was laboriously making her way up the steps, and as we neared the top, we squeezed past the street merchants with their wares displayed before them: combs and barrettes, loofah sponges, pens and pencils, and socks of every description.

At the top of the overpass, we paused to survey the street below that was choked with traffic. A cacophony of horns and vehicle noises mingled with the human ones that assaulted our ears. You not only had to be fleet of foot but deaf of ear to fully enjoy the bazaar scene.

There were shoe shops and dress shops and many places to buy house wares, their pots and pans and dish sets stacked out in front. There were carpenters sanding intricately carved chair legs, fabric and notion shops, and the tarboosh man working his press that heats and molds the felt to make the tasseled fezzes.

Abdou, a young shopkeeper, offered us a smoke on a sheesha pipe and some tea. He talked about being a secondary school science teacher who moonlighted in the family appliqué shop in the Street of the Tentmakers.

His grandfather, with over 70 years of sewing experience, still sat cross-legged on the dais and fashioned the intricate, appliquéd designs out of scraps of brightly colored cloth.

On the way to the Mausoleum of Sultan al-Ghuri, where the dervishes were to perform, our path was blocked by the effluent of a stopped-up drain and recent rain. No one wanted to chance falling into the sewage, even though it looked no more than ankle deep. We decided to play "follow the leader" as we followed a line of local Egyptians who were also going to watch the dervishes dance. We flattened ourselves and hugged the side of the building as our feet balanced on a ledge of stone. "Walk like an Egyptian," one of the persons ahead of us said with a grin, exhibiting that famous Egyptian wit and presenting us with images of two-dimensional hieroglyphs.

As we watched the evening's performance, our eyes were mesmerized as the dervishes' skirts became a kaleidoscope of color...red, yellow, green, and blue. The dervishes were Sufis who believed that they could achieve mystical communion with God and be transported to spiritual ecstasy through their whirling dances. Faster and faster the men whirled to the drum beats until I felt dizzy just watching them. Soon the dervishes became spinning tops that twirled and whirled until at last they stopped, their faces glistening with sweat. The dancers' steps were hypnotic and showed us a side of Egypt we had never seen. Recollecting our experiences that evening, I was reminded of my first encounter with the "real" Egypt there in the street.

The vendor was right. I dropped it...my heart...in Egypt.[2]

§

Since our apartment on Road 11 was situated close to the shopping area of Road 9, we did our fruit and vegetable shopping at the stalls along the street, although we did buy some of our staples like rice and tea at the corner store. Cairo merchants were notorious for not having spare change for their customers after their purchases were tallied. According to the merchants, the Central Bank of Egypt did not print enough money, so the merchants had to scrounge for small bills, and they would often expect the customers to produce exact change for their purchases.

I've never seen grubbier bills than the ones we saw in Egypt. The pound notes were small and usually crumpled, having been stuffed into

---

[2] First published in *AAA Going Places* March/April 1999

galabiyya pockets. They had changed hands so many times that it was often difficult to distinguish one note from another. The color for most currency had long since faded to a sweaty, nondescript brown, and you didn't really want to wonder where the notes had been. To counter this problem of short change, one proprietor on Road 9 started giving small change in the form of sticks of gum, Chicklets, and matchsticks. It seemed like an ingenious response to the lack of small bills, but I never knew what to do when I was handed a handful of Chicklets. Should one eat them? It seemed pretty risky.

It was only later in discussing the lack of change situation with another newly-arrived American that I learned about her response to the situation. She had figured out the equivalent currency of a matchstick, a Chicklet, and a stick of gum and had started a collection of her own. When she went to Road 9 and tried to pay for her purchases with Chicklets, matchsticks, and gum, the owner of the shop was incensed. The American couldn't understand why the shop owner wouldn't take the very change he had dispensed, and her reasoning was that if it was good for the goose, it was good for the gander.

We did most of our souvenir shopping on Road 9, where we bought beautiful inlaid wood and mother of pearl boxes, Egyptian perfume bottles with stoppers shaped like Turkish minarets, cartouches that spelled out our name in hieroglyphs, and mud clay figures of everyday Egyptian life. One of our favorite treasures is a clay-mud lamp in the shape of a coffee shop with patrons on the roof playing chess and reading the newspaper. There are even two "bouncers" standing in front of the coffee shop, which is named Sugar Street, after Nagib Mafouz's famous book.

It was on Road 9 where our favorite Mexican restaurant was located. The establishment served breakfast, but we soon learned that if you wanted pancakes, you'd have to bring your own syrup because the pancakes came with a drizzle of molasses. Maple syrup was not available in Egypt at that time.

Intricately carved chairs and tables spilled out in front of a carpenter's shop where we bought our mashribeyya coffee table that was edged with a lattice of wooden pegs of five different shapes. The carving art of mashribeyya was a traditional art form used in windows and doors, especially in the harem. Women could peer out from the lattice-work screen to the street below and still be protected from prying eyes. Mashribeyya also helped to cool the hot desert air as it passed over the latticework.

The weather was hot and dry as you would expect in a desert country, but the heat was more tolerable than the humid heat we experienced in Pakistan. It seldom rained, maybe once or twice a year, so everything was covered with a fine film of dust and dirt. On occasions when it did rain, we learned not to walk under trees, for our clothes would soon be splotched with ink-like spots of brown as the rain drops rolled down the dirty leaves.

Our apartment came equipped with roll-down metal grates over the windows to prevent the gritty, fine-as-dust sand from seeping into the apartment. Despite the use of these grates, dust and dirt would still coat every surface in the apartment, especially during the Khamsin, that 50-day period in April and May when sandstorms carried on oppressively hot winds would roll in from the Western Sahara desert. Our first glimpse of a Khamsin was spectacular as we watched the sky become a yellow-brownish color in the west. You had to be vigilant in rolling down all the grates before the wind started to howl and the sand made small, tinkling sounds as it hit the glass windows. Gradually, small heaps of grit formed alongside the cracks under the doors and under the windows.

One Khamsin was especially memorable for the blackness of the sky, and it reminded us of the Dust Bowl in the 30s in the Plains of the Midwest. Some Egyptians even thought that the world was ending, and reports to that effect appeared in the local papers the next day.

Cairo was notorious for its poor air quality, and the air we breathed contained ten times the World Health Organization's recommendation for pollutants and particulate matter. We lived in Ma'adi, halfway between the burning garbage dumps near the Moqattam Hills and the cement factories in Helwan. Depending on which way the wind blew, you got a lung full of smoke from the burning garbage dumps or cement dust from the factories. Compounding the situation was the exhaust from the crush of cars and trucks that plied the roads. At the time the Egyptian Government was seeking ways to eliminate lead from gasoline, so people would at least not be exposed to high levels of lead poisoning from the air they breathed.

I had a rash of health problems and suffered from recurring sinus infections, which necessitated taking more antibiotics than I wanted to. Surprisingly, the boys were now outgrowing their asthma, for which we were extremely grateful. We had been told by our allergist in Lewiston, Idaho that if a child acquires asthma before puberty, he usually outgrows it by the time he reaches adulthood. My sinus problems cleared up immediately whenever we traveled by train to Alexandria, which fronted the Mediterranean Sea and was bathed in the salty, marine air.

Unfortunately, my sinus congestion would return upon arrival in Cairo. Over the course of four years, I learned that if I ventured downtown or went exploring in the Khan el Khalili, I would suffer for my outing, and it would take me a week to clear out my sinuses.

Cairo had a population of 17 million, three million who commuted in and out of the city for their jobs. It seemed incredible that the city with such poor infrastructure would function with that many people, but somehow it did. We credited the city's ability to function to its occupants' good-natured humor, and we rarely saw verbal confrontations or fisticuffs among the Egyptians.

Traffic in the city was daunting for the tangle of cars and trucks as well as the deafening horn honking. It seemed that a Cairene could drive without lights, but he could not drive without his horn. Drivers regularly made six lanes of traffic out of three, and we soon learned that traffic signals were merely "suggestions" to stop. One paid no attention to red lights, only to traffic policemen, who stood on a raised pedestal in the middle of intersections while waving their arms and tooting their whistles. The key to driving in Cairo was to fill a hole in the traffic ahead or adjacent to you.

We ordered a factory-direct car from Japan when we first arrived, but with factory delays and paperwork snafus, at the end of six months in country, we were still without a car. We had been able to get around the city by walking, taking the subway, taking the shuttle to work, and taking taxis. We figured that since we had gotten along without a car for six months, we wouldn't need one. There was only one occasion where we would regret that decision.

Our son, Brian, was a freshman in high school at Cairo American College, where he took drama class. He was horsing around one day in class when he landed directly on the marble floor, dislocating his kneecap and forcing it to the side of his leg. I received a call from the school nurse saying that Brian had fallen and that I needed to get him to the hospital. The school had called the hospital and had arranged for one of the local orthopedic surgeons to meet us there. I flagged down a taxi and raced to the school nurse's office, where I called Tim and asked him to meet us at the hospital.

Brian was in a lot of pain, but he had had the foresight after he had fallen to pop his kneecap back in place. The doctor after manipulating Brian's knee, told us Brian would not require surgery but would be put in a cast from his ankle to his hip to allow for the healing process to take place. Apparently, injuries such as Brian's often heal when the dislocation occurs for the first time.

We had to figure out how to get our son, a six-foot tall kid with a cast from his ankle to his hip, to school and back for the next six weeks. It was not an easy task because Brian couldn't get up the steps of the school bus, and we didn't have a car. We decided to arrange for taxi service twice a day, and I walked down to Road 9 to the dispatcher's kiosk to make arrangements.

Yes, they would arrange for a taxi to pick Brian up and take him to school and back home. That plan worked in theory but not in practice. As it turned out, the fare of three Egyptian pounds was not a big incentive, and if the taxi driver could find a passenger who wanted to go downtown at a fare of 20 pounds, he would of course take the 20-pound fare. After numerous instances when the taxi driver didn't show up at either end, I became angry and stomped down to the dispatcher's kiosk to give him a piece of my mind.

I shouted at the dispatcher and told him of the inconvenience of not having the taxi driver appear at our home or at school. Although I felt better after my tirade, ultimately, it didn't improve our situation one bit. The encounter turned out not to be my finest hour of intercultural communication. The taxi driver's appearance was still hit-and-miss at best.

After a few days of Brian's being late to school, I learned to eat crow, an acquired taste in my mind, one that was not entirely palatable. I decided that a softer approach might work better, so I baked a batch of chocolate brownies, marched down to the dispatcher's office, and presented the brownies to the dispatcher, who shared them with the taxi drivers sitting in his kiosk. I apologized for my previous tirade, and I indicated that we would be willing to pay a higher fare for taxi service if it was dependable. This approach worked much better than the previous one, but still we lamented our decision not to buy a vehicle. Getting a six-foot kid in the back seat of a taxi was not an easy task. Brian had to sit sideways with his casted leg straight out. We discovered that the Soviet-built Lada taxis, which were so prevalent in Cairo, were not wide enough, and the doors would not close on one side or the other. The only taxi that would work was the French Peugeot, which was bigger and more expensive to operate.

Most of the taxi drivers who drove Ladas also lived on a shoestring, and their taxis were held together with the proverbial baling wire and chewing gum. More times than not, we would have to advance our taxi driver the fare so he could stop at the petrol station for enough petrol to get us where we needed to go.

§

About this time, I grew concerned that our Pakistani cat, George, was getting increasingly lonely because he was the only one of his species in our apartment; he could no longer go outside due to the rabies problem that was prevalent in the city. Periodically, the Egyptian police would patrol at night and shoot the strays they found on the streets in an effort to reduce rabies in the city. It was difficult to find medical care for the human population, let alone the animal population.

Our Regional Medical Officer had warned all Americans not to pet any stray animal on the street, but I defied his orders and became determined to find George a mate, one that would become the love of his life.

She was a scrawny thing, a small black and white kitten that mewed piteously beside the guard shack of our building. My heart went out to her, even before I knew she was a female cat because she was black and white, and she looked like she completed the other end of my concept of two black and white bookends.

After I spied the kitten, I went upstairs to find a box to put her in. I prayed, "Lord, if you want me to have this kitten, please let her be there when I come back down." When I returned to the ground floor, she was nowhere to be found, and despite my prayer seeking God's approval of my plan, I set about finding her. I even enlisted the help of the Egyptian guard and asked him (in Arabic) to help me locate her. We finally found her cowering underneath a parked car in the parking lot. I brought her upstairs to our apartment to assess her situation. She was the scrawniest cat I had ever seen, and her fur was dirty and matted, but she looked at me with such trusting green eyes. I called the local vet, who came to the house to give her a well-kitty check. He sexed her and told us she was female and approximately four months of age.

We started feeding her and were amazed at the amount of food she could consume. She ate and ate and before long, her tummy started dragging on the ground. Her little legs were not long enough to support her massive mid-section. Concerned, I called the vet to ask him how to prevent her from eating herself to death. He said we should put the food where she could reach it three times a day and that gradually, she would become accustomed to knowing food would always be available. At four months of age, she had been living on the streets and had been literally starving to death.

We called her Katmandu and nicknamed her Kaydu for short. After a few months we introduced her to George, who snarled and hissed at the black and white ball of fur. Although Kaydu did not become the love of George's life, they grew to tolerate each other. We surmised that George at five years of age was already an elder statesman, and he found it difficult to tolerate the feisty kitten. Because he was such a gentlemanly cat, he allowed Kaydu to eat first, and although they didn't curl up together, they became companions to each other. Kaydu became my kitty, for she recognized that I was the one who rescued her from a life of deprivation on the streets of Cairo. She had won the kitty lottery.

§

Both of our sons loved attending Cairo American College, CAC, the American-funded international school located in Ma'adi. We discovered that international schools had the best of both worlds for their small student body, low student-to-teacher ratio, highly-educated parent population, good funding by the U.S. government, and excellent teachers.

Students had a large number of extracurricular activities to choose from, and our boys took full advantage of the offerings. Both Brian and Scott were involved in It's Academic and Model U.N. and traveled to regional cities to compete in academic competitions. Scott was co-captain of the Junior Varsity basketball team and traveled to Amman, Jordan and Kuwait to play in tournaments with other schools in the Middle Eastern conference. Brian was in drama and traveled to London with his drama class to see Shakespearean plays performed by professional actors. Both boys were members of the Poetry Club, and they would meet with other students to read and discuss poetry. The eighth graders' graduation trip was a week-long trip to the Sinai to explore the desert. Funding the boys' extracurricular trips became difficult, and we finally had to restrict the boys to one or at the most, two trips per year.

Although we enjoyed all the pluses to living the overseas life, we keenly felt the downsides as well. We felt cut off from our families because of the long distances between us. Home leaves and R & Rs somehow did not make up for missing all those important family events that had taken place without us. The following article relates our mixed feelings about our vagabond USAID lifestyle.

In Cairo, Making Memories

As I made the bed this morning and fluffed the pillow into place, I was reminded of my grandmother. For this had been my grandmother's pillow, then my mother's, and now mine. My grandmother raised and plucked the geese for the down and feather pillow herself, then covered it with a cheery rose floral ticking. I had just rescued it from 40 years of sleep in humid Wisconsin summers; now its ticking was sweat-stained and yellowed. I had tucked the pillow into our household effects with the intent of getting it re-ticked in our next post. Now, in Cairo, where I had had it recovered, I sleep on it every night, aware of all the family memories it recalls.

The images of Grandma that come to mind are of an elderly woman who kept an entryway wall covered with her grandchildren's artwork. I remember the old-fashioned black telephone that hung in the parlor and sleeping in Grandma's bed, where I continually rolled downhill into the permanent trough where grandma slept.

The funny thing about Grandma was that she became better looking as she aged. Earlier pictures showed her as haggard, her hooked nose the most striking feature of her face. Grandma's nose had an extra function: It could touch her chin when she took her teeth out, something she did often to entertain my sister and me.

I remember coming home from a weekend at Grandma's house with my long hair in a ponytail slicked back with Alberto VO5. My sister and I always reeked of the stuff, and the first thing Mother would do was to wash our hair. The last image I have of Grandma is also of hair, but instead of her doing my hair, I am combing hers. I am 15, and she is lying on the couch wasting away from stomach cancer.

As a parent of two middle-school-aged boys, I sometimes wonder if we are not doing our children a disservice with our vagabond lifestyle. Sure, we give them all the advantages our type of life affords: They become bilingual, or perhaps even trilingual. They know what it's like to ride camels at the base of the Pyramids or see a pride of lions up close. They've been to Jerusalem, home of three of the world's religions, and have traveled the Silk Road in the footsteps of Alexander the Great and Genghis Khan.

I wonder if they will have the same kind of memories of their grandparents that I have of mine. Will they remember their grandma for her twinkly blue eyes and her scrumptious apple pie? Will they remember being shown Grandpa's latest invention in a two-car garage piled so high with junk that there was barely space to walk, let alone store a car? Will they remember that Grandpa helped bait their hooks the first time they went fishing? Given such little time spent with their grandparents, will they have any memories at all?

I have two close friends who are good at making memories. They have a special knack of making gatherings of friends and family meaningful. They celebrate holidays with many decorations; as soon as one holiday is over, up go the decorations for the next. They give small gifts spontaneously, sometimes for no reason at all.

I think Foreign Service families need to make special efforts to keep ties with relatives far away. We need to help our children develop a talent for writing letters and for writing down thoughts that can be cherished again and again. We need to keep pictures close at hand so that the faces that are dear to us are not forgotten by our children. Like my two friends, we need to do things not just to occupy time, but to make memories for ourselves and our children. Most of all, I want my boys to be able to pick up some small memento from their grandparents and be able to say, "Remember when...?"[3]

§

During a four-year posting, USAID families are allowed to go on home leave after the second year and are encouraged to spend that time in the U.S. reorienting themselves to the American way of life. Every two years employees' families can ship back to post at government expense, 500 lbs. of air freight for a family of four. Most expats use this time and weight allowance to shop for their kids' clothing and shoes, toys, books, hobby items, and any other things that they can't get at post – chocolate chips, for example.

We thought we were being so practical by choosing a freight forwarder that was headquartered in Portland, Oregon, where our families lived and where we usually went on home leave. The thought was if we had problems with the shipment, we could easily communicate with the shipper. Little did we foresee that this particular shipment would be the one that caused the most heartache.

I typed the following article as I sat at the computer with tears coursing down my cheeks. I pounded on the keyboard and peered at the screen

---

[3] First published in *The Foreign Service Journal* January 1995
Republished in <u>The Foreign Service Reader, Selected Articles from 77 Years of the Foreign Service Journal,</u> AFSA and DACOR, 1997

through watery eyes. We had been through the frustration of not being able to trace our lost shipment even though we had communicated with all the shippers at each leg of our air freight's journey. Each of those shippers claimed they were not the last to have seen or been responsible for our boxes. Ultimately, after having amassed a two-inch file of shipping documents, we had to admit our air freight was lost. The following article, published in *The Foreign Service Journal*, was partly responsible for someone from USAID Washington's shipping department coming to Cairo to investigate lost freight. Although we never recovered our shipment, I received some satisfaction by seeing my article in print.

The Lessons of Air Freight in Cairo

There's a lesson to be learned when your air freight doesn't arrive, but I'm not sure what it is. Is it, "Patience is a virtue?" If so, I'd rather not be so virtuous. We were notified over a month ago that our air freight had been shipped and it was awaiting customs clearance. Last Thursday we waited all day for its arrival only to be told at 5 p.m. that the shipping documents had been cleared but not the actual freight — and one of the two boxes was missing.

I am pessimistic about ever actually seeing our air freight. After all, in Egypt the two most common Arabic words are *insha'Allah* (God willing) and *ma'alesh* (never mind). I'm afraid that in the six years we've lived overseas, I've been transformed from an optimist to a pessimist. As columnist George F. Will says, "The nice part about being a pessimist is that you are constantly being either proven right or pleasantly surprised."

Could the lesson be, "Good things come to those who wait?" Perhaps. We waited six months for another air freight shipment, shipped from Islamabad to Portland, Oregon, just before the Gulf War broke out in 1991. We were lucky since we were one of only three families to successfully ship out our air freight that we had packed before our hasty evacuation to the United States. Six months later, our air freight was found still languishing in London, after travelling around the globe at least once. The cold weather items for Oregon actually arrived back in Pakistan before us, where of course, they weren't needed.

Maybe the lesson learned is, "Do not store up for yourself treasures on earth." (Matthew 6:19 NIV) We've learned of the tyranny of things in our 23 years of marriage and in an almost equal number of moves. We were told upon entering the Foreign Service that we stood a good chance of losing all our material things sometime during our career and not to take overseas anything we couldn't live without. We decided to ignore that advice and take our chances. Sometimes familiar things make all the difference in a difficult adjustment to a new country.

Yet, I still was heartsick when the movers told me they could not locate our air freight box. It's not the monetary value that matters so much, but that some of those items would be difficult, if not impossible to replace. How can I replace the dozen different kinds of material I had painstakingly selected for the memory quilt I was stitching for our son? The fabrics were chosen in the colors and designs he liked best: teal blue, purple, and black, with nautical scenes to commemorate his summer sailing trip, a book print to symbolize another interest, and several cat prints to remind him of our cherished pet.

Our youngest son had shipped his size 13 basketball shoes in the air freight because they were too big to fit in his carry-on luggage. You know, the kind endorsed by some NBA star – shoes that allow a kid to slam-dunk a 10-foot basketball hoop. His old shoes have soles that are semi-detached, held together with Shoe-Goo. When his English teacher tired of seeing him flapping around and asked if he was going to get a new pair of shoes, he replied, "They're in the air freight." His shrug said it all. If you have kids with big feet, you know how impossible it is to find size 13 shoes at most overseas posts.

But maybe the lesson to be learned is, "The squeaky wheel gets the grease." We're trying to tread the thin line between the squeaky wheel and the ugly American while keeping our shipping problem in the forefront of people's minds. *Insha'Allah*, the lost will be found. If, on the other hand, it's been stolen, I just hope that whoever has stolen it will enjoy it as much as we would have.[4]

§

We were fortunate to be able to travel extensively throughout Egypt during our four-year posting – to the Sinai on a Community Liaison Office (CLO) bus trip; to Siwa, an oasis in the Western Desert; to the Suez Canal on the Teddy Roosevelt, an American aircraft carrier; to Wadi el Natrun, where we visited 5th-century churches and monasteries; and to the Nile on a CLO-sponsored cruise.

---

[4]   First published in *The Foreign Service Journal* January 1995

The Nile cruise was a bargain for its price of approximately $250 per person for the week-long cruise as well as bus transfers and flights to Abu Simbel, where massive Egyptian monuments had been relocated in preparation for the building of the High Aswan Dam in the 1960s. The cruise was inexpensive because there had been recent terrorist attacks on Hatshetsup's Temple near Luxor, which had killed dozens of foreign tourists, and the Egyptian economy was reeling from the attacks. Tourism plummeted and foreign residents in-country were able to take advantage of the incredible deal. Not only did we receive a remarkable price, but we had additional security on board to safeguard the Americans due to the threat of additional terrorist strikes.

It was on the Nile cruise that we discovered the charm of Aswan, home of the High Aswan Dam, a remarkable feat of engineering. The following is an article I wrote about the romanticism I felt on being in the same spot where Agatha Christie wrote <u>Death on the Nile</u>.

Tea with Agatha Christie

It was spring in Egypt in 1995 and Tim and I had been working hard to the point of burnout, so we decided to book a long weekend in Aswan, the historic Nubian city on the Nile south of Cairo, just a short distance upstream from the First Cataract and up the river from the site of the Aswan Dam. The Old Cataract Hotel, which was built in the colonial era intrigued us, but we knew that we probably couldn't afford the rates. It was, after all, a hotel frequented by Victorian travelers on the Grand Tour and made famous by the likes of Agatha Christie and Winston Churchill. Never mind. We could book a room in the New Cataract Hotel, built as a high rise on the same property along the Nile, next to the Corniche and its promenade, and still enjoy the amenities of the old hotel. My goal was to have tea on the terrace where Agatha Christie is said to have penned her book, <u>Death on the Nile</u>.

We arrived late afternoon, and because we were so tired, both of us promptly fell asleep for two hours, waking up just as the sun was sinking lower on the horizon. We hurried to the terrace of the old hotel on the edge of the Nile and marveled at the setting we were now a part of. From the height of the terrace, we watched as the feluccas with their white nibbed fountain pen sails tacked their way down the river in the cool evening breeze. The Nile in the setting sun was a brilliant blue that contrasted sharply with the golden sand dunes on the opposite side of the river. In the foreground, the fuchsia bougainvillea spilled over the terrace and formed a perfect frame for this postcard scene.

Perched atop the sand dunes was St. Simeon, an ancient monastery, from where early desert Fathers departed to make converts to Christianity among the Nubians. Aswan marks the boundary between the Arab north and the African south. The city is legendary from earliest antiquity for its history and appears in writings by the Alexandrian geographer Eratosthenes. Aswan was the site of important measuring tools, nilometers, which marked the yearly flooding of the Nile that replenished the fellaheen's (farmers') fields with life-giving silt. The area was also the staging ground for the conquest of Sudan and the defeat of the Mahdi by the Anglo-Egyptian forces. We could literally feel the seep of history into our bones.

Elephantine Island, seen to the left in our view from the terrace, was dubbed that for the shape of its huge black rocks, which resembled a herd of elephants. All the colors of a perfect tableau were there: the black rocks of the island against the blue of the Nile; the gold of the sand spilling close to the water's edge; the white of the felucca sails; the chestnut brown skin of the Nubian servers. We were still in the Arab world but straddling the border with Africa.

"Ana ayza teh minfadlak." "I'd like some tea, please," I told the waiter in Arabic. After one year of twice a week Arabic language classes, taxi Arabic as I called it, I could speak simple phrases, bargain in Arabic to let the merchant know that I was a resident and not just a tourist, and get myself where I wanted to go. I made sure to use the "ak" ending for addressing men rather than the "ik" ending reserved for women. The tea arrived in a pot with porcelain cups and saucers, along with a dainty tea spoon for stirring the milk and sugar. Egyptians liked their tea and coffee overwhelmingly sweet and sometimes even held a cube of sugar between their front teeth while sipping their tea.

It was all so elegant, and I felt privileged to be there in that historic setting, but I also felt curiously out of place, almost like an imposter. I could have been sitting in the very spot where Agatha Christie wrote her novel. Did she sit at the same table in the wicker chairs on the south side of the terrace next to the carved wooden railing? Was she served by like Nubian servers, attired in white tunics with billowy pantaloons and soutache-embroidered vests? What did she order? Did she write studiously on pads of paper, madly scribbling as Hercule Poirot solved the murders aboard the *SS Sudan,* the sternwheeler that was the setting for the novel? How many hours of the day did she occupy a seat on the terrace?

As I drank my tea I pondered these questions. I fingered the porcelain tea cup and nibbled on the butter cookies that accompanied the tea. I believe we asked for a refill of hot water for our tea pot, for we didn't want to leave the terrace while there was still some light in the sky. We wanted to take in the amazing sights and the fragrance of the dry desert air before reluctantly leaving our table. I was consoled by the fact that there was always tomorrow and another opportunity for tea on the terrace, for exploring the ancient Nubian bazaar second only to Cairo's Khan el Khalili, for discovering untold treasures in the dusty shops that lined the rabbit warren of streets, and for inhaling the intoxicating mix of incense and spices. There was always tomorrow.

§

Surprisingly, Egyptians were among the people most open to discussing our religious beliefs while comparing them to their own. Muslims consider Christians to be People of the Book because we share a common belief in one God, whom they call Allah. Jews are also People of the Book, and Muslims and Jews as well as Christians share a common heritage in the person of Abraham, the Father of Nations.

I was curious hearing my students in Cairo relate their belief that Jesus was born under a coconut palm, not in a stable in Bethlehem. They were certain of this. I felt that we were living much closer to biblical history in Cairo than in any other location we lived. Just down the street from our apartment building on the Corniche, the road paralleling the Nile, was a church where Moses had been found in the bulrushes by Pharaoh's daughter. We visited the churches in Mar Girguis, where Joseph, Mary, and Baby Jesus sheltered on their Flight into Egypt. We sailed in a felucca on the Nile, which had once been turned into blood in retribution for Pharaoh's hardening of his heart in his refusal to let the Israelites go. We also experienced first-hand the plethora of flies that buzzed and settled everywhere – on food and on our bodies. These flies must have descended from the flies that had harassed the Egyptians as part of the Plagues visited upon them.

In the Sinai desert, we visited St. Catherine's Monastery and the Burning Bush, where Moses was instructed to remove his shoes because in coming face-to-face with God, he was standing on holy ground. We also saw Jethro's Well, where Moses would draw water for the flocks of goats he shepherded for forty years. Tim climbed the massive stone steps to the top of Mt. Sinai, where Moses received the Ten Commandments, which had been inscribed by God on stone tablets.

We were given the opportunity to overnight on board an American aircraft carrier, the Teddy Roosevelt, and experience the vastness of the Suez Canal, which leads into the Red Sea. This was the sea Moses parted in the Israelites' flight from Egypt. Were the chariots of Pharaoh's army still resting at the bottom of it?

Tim's Egyptian colleague, Ninette, her brother, Nabil, and their mother, whom I called simply Maman, the French word for mother, served as our guides as we ventured into Wadi el Natrun, The Valley of Natron, just west of the desert road leading from Cairo to Alexandria. Maman had been schooled in the French school system in Egypt before Egypt nationalized in the 1950s and spoke Arabic, her native language, and French but not English. In order to communicate with Maman, I tried my best to resurrect my long-rusty college French, which I hadn't spoken for 30 years. Somehow it worked.

Wadi el Natrun had at one time sheltered over 50 monasteries and housed hundreds of Coptic monks, who secreted themselves in their hermitage cells and prayed in devotion to God. These 5th and 6th century monasteries had walls eight-feet thick and massive drawbridges that could be drawn up in defense against the Bedouin raiders who came to the desert area to plunder and make converts to Islam at the point of a sword. Some of the monasteries and churches still stood as bulwarks of the Coptic faith for Coptic Christians.

After centuries of Christian asceticism, there are four monasteries in Wadi el Natrun that thrive today. We visited several of them and stepped back in time as we crossed the drawbridge into the courtyard within. Our guide was a monk garbed in a long, black robe with a hood embroidered with 13 white crosses, representing Christ and his 12 Apostles. He sported a bushy black beard and glasses and surprisingly, spoke with an American accent. He mentioned that one of his jobs was to update the monastery's computer system. Somehow, what our eyes beheld and our ears heard did not compute with where we were standing in an ancient monastery, dating from the 5th century. We felt a disconnect in this time warp we were encountering.

§

Because Tim was a U.S. Government employee, our family had access to the Army Post Office mail system, through which we received mail twice a week. We felt fortunate to have access to APO, and we knew that other Americans, some of whom were contractors, did not have the same privileges we had. It took approximately two weeks to receive and send mail, and we were able to order items such as shoes and clothing through mail order catalogs. Despite having access to APO, it wasn't without its drawbacks. The following article is one I wrote after weeks of frustration in dealing with JC Penney through our APO mail system.

Living in the Mythical Land of APO

I don't know if your experiences have mirrored ours, but dealing with mail order companies and creditors over the years using our Army Post Office (APO) or pouch addresses has been extremely frustrating. The average person stateside does not understand how the system works no matter how many times it has been explained to him. APO or pouch zip codes also do not fit within the computer scheme of many business firms. Here are a few examples of our (mis)communication with these companies:

From Reader's Digest: Congratulations! You (fill in the blank) Mr. Anderson have just been chosen among the select few within your (fill in the blank) Alaskan zip code to be a finalist in the third and final phase of our $5,000,000 giveaway. You may already have won the home of your dreams in your city, (fill in the blank) APO.

From a customer billing representative with AT & T: "I'm sorry, but we don't mail billings to overseas addresses." AT & T arbitrarily changed our zip code to an incorrect one, which resulted in our not receiving any bills for six months. They assumed we were skip artists and revoked our AT & T card.

From a billing clerk at the University of Oregon Health Sciences Center: "I'm sorry, but APO AE doesn't fit into our city and state computer configuration for addresses. Couldn't your mother forward the bill to you? Couldn't you rent a post office box to receive the bill?"

From the Postmaster in Olympia, Washington: "I'm sorry, but we can't insure mail going to Egypt." Whenever I'm in the Pacific Northwest, I now drive the extra 15 miles to little, podunk Tenino, Washington where the on-the-ball postmaster knows how to handle APO mail.

The following is a dialogue we had with JC Penney over a seven-month period regarding the incorrect change of address, which JC Penney arbitrarily instituted:

JC Penney, January 17: "We note you have moved and want to welcome you to your new home. The credit terms in your new state of residence are different from those that applied to your account where you previously resided..."

The Andersons, January 27: "For some reason JC Penney sends its catalogs to our correct address and monthly billings to a recently contrived, unknown address. The address listed above is our proper address, both for catalogs and billings."

The Andersons, April 2: "Our previous letter of January 27 advised JC Penney that our billings have been going astray. Do you contract out your billing services to someone outside of JC Penney? If so, please ensure that the address is corrected as follows..."

JC Penney, April 9: "We note you have moved and want to welcome you..."

JC Penney, April 16: "We note you have moved and want to welcome you..."

The Andersons, April 17: "This is the third correspondence I have had with JC Penney regarding an error in our mailing address. Please note that I have not moved in the past two and one-half years. I did not authorize JC Penney to change my address. The correct address should read..."

JC Penney, May 6: "Please accept our sincere apologies for the inconveniences you have experienced as a result of an incorrect zip code... We do have your correct zip code on record now and we will monitor your billings for several months...As a small token of our appreciation, we are enclosing a $10 gift certificate..."

JC Penney, May 21: "We note you have moved and want to welcome you..."

The Andersons, June 10: "Dear Ms. Furr: Thank you for your letter of May 6 and for addressing our address/billing problem. I also appreciate receiving the gift certificate, but would appreciate even more having the zip code problem resolved...Because I live in a third-world country known for its 5,000 year-old bureaucratic system, I expect delays and frustrations. I don't expect the same in dealing with U.S. companies. I remain optimistic that this problem will be resolved..."

JC Penney, July 13: Welcome to your new home! Enclosed is the Credit Account Agreement for the state in which you now live..."

JC Penney, July 18: "Ms. Anderson, please accept our sincere apologies for this unfortunate situation. We are making every effort to make a permanent change in our system to keep your address as you informed us... Recently there was a new implementation in the "standardization" program used to verify addresses. Hopefully this will improve our ability to keep records accurate and improve customer service..."

To JC Penney's credit, seven months later, they now have our correct zip code. I will tell you if and when we win the home of our dreams in our city, (fill in the blank) APO.[5]

§

Life continued as our boys grew into adolescents. They were now in middle school and high school – Brian as a freshman and Scott as an eighth grader. We keenly felt the opposing tugs of home and family contrasted with our life and contentment overseas. We had been overseas for seven years and rarely saw our families back home except during the summer while on R & R or home leave. Although we received letters regularly from home, it was not the same as being there to take part in weddings, birthdays, Christmas holidays, and other important family events.

We knew that my father had been growing increasingly forgetful, which both my mother and sister outlined in their letters from home. My sister was handicapped and lived over a hundred miles away from our parents, and although she could be there as a sounding board for my mother, it was difficult for my sister to make the long drive and help my parents cope with my father's physical and mental limitations.

Every son or daughter goes through pain and grief when elderly parents face end-of-life issues, but the circumstances and emotions associated with that process can be exacerbated when you're overseas and half way around the world from your family. The following article relates my experiences in returning to Portland to help my parents deal with my dad's Alzheimer's. It was the most difficult thing I have ever done, and I wasn't prepared for it. The second article is the eulogy I gave at my father's memorial service. The eulogy also includes a poem that Brian, our oldest son, wrote for his grandfather.

---

[5] First published on the Associates of American Foreign Service Worldwide (AAFSW) Web site

How Do You Like Them Apples?

Alzheimer's is such a cruel disease.

It was the summer of 1996 and I had just flown back to Portland, Oregon with our son, Scott, who was 14. We stayed a few days with Grandma and Grandpa so Scott could get to know them better and be spoiled by Grandma. She warned him that she was going to get all her hugs and kisses in while she could, so he'd better be prepared. Scott grinned his usual, freckle-faced grin. A basketball player at the age of 14, he towered over Grandma's 4'11". She's always said that she was just too short on one end.

Scott's good nature withstood the rigors of Grandpa's Alzheimer's, which manifested itself in forgetfulness, repetition of speech, inability to concentrate for more than 10-15 minutes, and agitation. Grandpa was taking medication for his agitation. It seemed to make him tired all the time, practically catatonic if he got too agitated and Grandma pushed the dosage, but tiredness was easier to cope with than agitation and verbal combativeness.

We chanced letting Scott "grandpa sit" so I could get Grandma away for some much-needed change of scenery. We went to a movie, out to lunch, and did some grocery shopping, although we were careful not to leave for more than two to three hours. Grandma used to go with a neighbor to do those things if they happened to coincide with Grandpa's nap. That came to a stop when the neighbors found Grandpa wandering off by himself down the street, not knowing where he was. They always brought him back, and for that, we were grateful. But, the neighbors' goodwill could only stretch so far, and Grandma knew she couldn't take advantage of the neighbors' kindnesses forever.

We soon learned that it was easier to live in Grandpa's reality than in our own in dealing with him. Because of Grandpa's short-term memory loss, conversations often bordered on the ridiculous.

"How do you like them apples?" Grandpa remarked from his easy chair as I stood looking out the small living room window overlooking the backyard.

"Yeah, Daddy, I can see those apples."

..."Punks (his nickname for me), have you seen all the apples on my trees out there?"

"Daddy, I can see them from here," I said as I stood by the window looking at the apple trees in the backyard. I tried adding some variety to the conversation: "What kind of apples are they?" (I knew that there was one red delicious, one yellow delicious, and one gravenstein tree).

"I think we got a coupla delicious trees and one gravenstein."

Scott, who was sitting on the couch and had been listening to the conversation all along, became the focus of Grandpa's attention. "Hey Michael, have ya seen the trees out in the backyard?" Michael is one of his other grandsons.

"His name is Scott, Daddy."

Scott had been forewarned of Grandpa's illness and played along. By the end of his time with Grandma and Grandpa, he had been called four or five male names, even Bingo, after the dog.

Scott replied, "I can see them, Grandpa."

This conversation played itself out every 20 minutes or so, like a badly-scripted play. Sometimes the conversations varied with Grandpa convinced that he was in Wisconsin and that he wanted to go "home." We learned from the Alzheimer's Association seminar that this longing for home is very typical of Alzheimer's patients.

At first we tried to convince Grandpa that he was home, and this had been his home for over 25 years.

"Oh no, it ain't!" Grandpa's confusion and anger flashed in his eyes.

We also learned that swearing and the breakdown of inhibitions is common among Alzheimer's victims. Grandpa had worked on the docks as a ship fitter for over 20 years. In the best of times, his language was often blue; we tried to ignore the recent developments in his language as best we could. Grandma and I often squirmed when Grandpa tried to tell Scott off-color jokes.

Still, Grandpa could not be convinced that the house he was living in wasn't in Wisconsin.

"Well, if this ain't Eau Claire, how in the world did I get that bookcase in the living room?"

Grandpa was certain he remembered building the bookcase in his shop on Lexington Avenue in Eau Claire, Wisconsin. His voice retained the pride of an artisan, for he was still able to discern that the maple bookcase fit snugly into the corner of the living room. He designed it himself to fit the items displayed there.

"I'm going to get my keys and drive to Wisconsin."

Grandma and I tried every line of reasoning we could with Grandpa, but we couldn't convince him that Wisconsin was 2,000 miles away. For him, Wisconsin was home.

We never talked of Grandpa's illness in his presence because it only made him more agitated. Both Grandma and Grandpa were of the generation that didn't talk of those things. They also blindly accepted what the doctor said and didn't ask questions. The doctor treated Grandpa's symptoms, but in my opinion, never got to the root cause. Perhaps I was being unfair to the doctor, and his part in this horrible play could be reasonably excused: he was part of an HMO and the HMO was calling the shots; he only had so much time to spend with each patient; if he ordered tests for Grandpa, it meant that fewer tests and treatment could be given to his other patients, and perhaps there really was nothing that could be done for Alzheimer's; Grandpa was a difficult patient in the best of circumstances.

"Nobody's messing with my head!" Grandpa would thunder when either Grandma or I suggested there might be medication that could help his condition. Nobody held out the hope of Aricept, a medication for Alzheimer's, in Grandpa's case. We learned from the Alzheimer's Association that there were over 100 illnesses that manifested themselves in memory loss, some of which were treatable. In any event, treatment was not suggested. My mother remembered the doctor saying early on in Grandpa's illness: "Can you imagine the time we're going to have when Hans needs to go into a nursing home?"

I drove Scott to Moscow, Idaho so he could spend the rest of the summer with his best buddy, Ty. My rationale was to foster fond memories of Grandpa for Scott; these issues of disease and the diminishing of Grandpa's faculties were matters that were too weighty for a 14-year-old. These were adult worries.

When I returned from Moscow to Portland, Oregon, Grandma, Grandpa, and I settled into a fairly predictable pattern of daily concerns. I empathized with my mom, for I began to see the awful 24-hours-a-day stress this disease expected of you. Much as an infant does, Grandpa began to mix his days and nights. He took long naps and awakened at two or three in the morning, ready to start the day. If we kept him from napping, he became difficult. He would turn the TV on too loudly and would plug the coffee pot in, sometimes burning it dry. Lack of sleep and the threat of fire became all too real for Grandma and me.

Grandpa neglected his hygiene and it became all but impossible to get him into the shower more than once a week. He gave up shaving unless Grandma badgered him about it. Part of his hygiene problem stemmed from his reduced mobility. It was difficult to get him in and out of the shower and we feared he would fall. Grandpa outweighed Grandma by 100 pounds.

He dribbled on his chin and shirt when he ate, and his eating habits became increasingly erratic. This was consistent with the information the Alzheimer's Association dispensed about the course of the disease. Because the disease affects the appetite center of the brain, patients go on binges and have cravings for strange combinations of foods: ketchup on toast, for example. Conversely, Alzheimer's victims may give up eating entirely, or eat only sporadically. Grandpa went through both phases. For a time, Grandpa craved sugary foods and gobbled everything in sight. Because he couldn't remember having eaten, Grandpa noshed practically around the clock. An offshoot of Grandpa's eating habits was that the dog, Bingo, became pretty porky. Grandpa had to feed his buddy every time he took a bite, and of course, Bingo loved being fed. We gave up telling Grandpa that he had just eaten because we couldn't stop him.

Part of Alzheimer's is the paranoia that most patients exhibit. Grandma and I took Grandpa down to the Department of Motor Vehicles so Grandpa could fail the written driver's test for the fifth time. He wasn't able to understand the test directions and marked every item for every question of the multiple-choice test. Somehow it was easier to let Grandpa think the DMV was out to "get" him than persuade him to give up driving. He was also convinced that the wrecker outside the tavern, where he totaled their second vehicle rammed him on purpose. In truth, the policeman found Grandpa very disoriented and brought him home to Grandma. Grandma hid the car keys and pretended she didn't know where they were. As Grandpa became more agitated, this failed, and we resorted to having a friend disable the distributor so if he found the keys, he couldn't hurt himself or anyone else. For most men with Alzheimer's, the inability to drive and the increasing dependency on others become the most contentious issues.

It was difficult to watch Grandpa's abilities slowly wither and die. He had always been a jack-of-all-trades and had built two houses all by himself, including logging the lumber for the houses with a team of horses. Now he could do nothing more than stare at all his tools in his tool sheds. We would send him out to the shed hoping he would put together a toolbox for each of his grandsons. He would wander back to the house in frustration realizing that this was something he had been able to do in the past.

We learned from the Alzheimer's Association that those afflicted with the disease do well with repetitive tasks. Grandpa was happiest when he was peeling apples or shelling nuts. It would keep him occupied for a full 10 or 15 minutes. He also enjoyed picking up apples from the ground and digging dandelions. Part of the exhaustion of the caregiver comes with having to plan tasks or activities in fifteen-minute increments to occupy the patient day in and day out.

Grandpa had always enjoyed reading, mostly *Popular Mechanic* magazines, *Country*, and *Reader's Digest*, but now, he spent less and less time at it. I watched as he went from reading whole articles to merely reading the captions under the pictures, and finally, to only looking at the pictures. He derived great pleasure from looking at old family photo albums and seemed to recognize most of the faces in the photos. For Grandpa, the past became more real than the present, and we often relived old memories with him.

Three days before Scott and I were to leave to return to Egypt, Grandpa's situation took a turn for the worst. He spent three hours in the blazing sun, trying in vain to start the car using every key on his key chain. We couldn't persuade him to come inside the house and cool down. He may have had a stroke, which further diminished his abilities because his condition declined rapidly after that. At that point, I decided I couldn't leave Grandma and Grandpa, and I set out to put in place a support system for their needs.

If what I have described so far sounds unbearably bleak, I have to admit there were moments of levity amid the tears as we dealt with the absurd. We also received heaps of blessings in the people who were sent our way. A frantic call on the day Grandpa's condition worsened triggered a visit by a social worker who became a godsend to us. She was of Swiss extraction, and my mother took to her immediately. The social service agency initiated a cleaning service for my mother whose own health was deteriorating. The home health care nurses who came to the house spread cheer as they monitored my father's health. The elder-law attorney we retained set up my mother's finances so she would not become destitute paying for Grandpa's future nursing home care. The pastor to seniors gave us hope in the midst of this overwhelming situation. Countless others shared their own experiences with Alzheimer's and let us know we weren't alone.

Grandma couldn't deal with the psychological burden of guilt in placing Grandpa in a nursing home, even though she was sacrificing her own health in caring for him. This is very common among families where Alzheimer's has struck. Two months after Scott and I returned to Cairo, Grandpa became incontinent and couldn't move his body so Grandma could change him. He lay in the wet bed all day. Grandma tried calling the neighbors repeatedly for help, and even 911, but no one was home to respond to her calls. The doctor finally came over after he finished work and lifted Grandpa out of the bed, changed the bed himself, and dressed Grandpa in clean clothing. The doctor took control of the situation; he absolved Grandma of the decision and decided that Grandpa needed to be placed in a nursing home. Grandma was greatly relieved, but she later came to the conclusion that the guilt she was feeling on seeing Grandpa in a nursing home was worse than the physical and mental exhaustion she suffered in caring for him.

Grandpa died three months after going into the nursing home. It was heartbreaking on the day of Grandpa's memorial service to hear Grandma tell Grandpa upon seeing his body that she would be joining him shortly. Grandma died a little over a year and a half later, two weeks before their 57th wedding anniversary. I think she didn't want to spend another anniversary apart.

§

The same summer I returned to Oregon to help my parents was the year that USAID experienced a Reduction in Force, (RIF), which required that the agency cut its American staff in Cairo by ten direct-hire employees. The situation was stressful because no one knew whose job would be cut, and we were notified six months prior to the actual RIF. Normally back home if the primary wage earner loses a job, it's stressful, but it doesn't always result in other losses. If you lose a job overseas, the whole family is affected by the upheaval and the relocation back to the States. It results in a loss of home, a loss of schools for the children, a loss of job for the spouse, and a loss of friends when the family repatriates to the States. During this time we had been feeling the stresses of the RIF compounded by various personal health problems. Were we anxious about our situation? Yes, because it was difficult to transcend our human nature. No, because we had confidence that whatever happened, God was in charge.

We lived in Egypt, the land of miracles - the Burning Bush, the Ten Commandments, and the parting of the Red Sea. Did we continue to experience miracles similar to those that Moses experienced in the very land where we were living? Yes and no. Yes, in that God heard our prayers and answered them. No, in that His answers were rarely flashy or conspicuous to anyone but us.

While in Egypt, God answered a prayer by directing me to the following poem, which comforted me:

Rejoice

In heavenly love abiding,
No change my heart shall fear;
And safe is such confiding,
For nothing changes here.
The storm may roar without me,
My heart may low be laid,
But God is round about me,
And can I be dismayed?

Wherever He may guide me,
No fear shall turn me back;
My Shepherd is beside me,
And nothing shall I lack.
His wisdom ever waketh,
His sight is never dim;
He knows the way He taketh,
And I will walk with Him.

Green pastures are before me,
Which yet I have not seen;
Bright skies will soon be o'er me,
Where darkest clouds have been.
My hope I cannot measure,
My path to life is free;
My Savior is my treasure,
And he will walk with me.

– Anna L. Waring

§

I had always been intrigued by what the Celts call "thin places," areas on earth where the separation between the Divine and humanity is thinner, where humans can get closer to God and feel His presence. The early Christian Celts believed that only three feet separated heaven and earth, and a thin place was where the distance had been lessened. I had several years earlier attended two Celtic Christianity retreats at our church's retreat center in Lost River, West Virginia, and I liked how the early Celts worshiped God. I felt they had a more holistic approach to God, and they worshiped Him in every facet of their life – from their rising in the morning to their laying down for the night. There was no separation between the body and the spirit as in Greek beliefs, some of which had been adopted into our present-day Christian practices.

As I learned more about Celtic Christianity at these retreats, I read their prayers of devotion, which expressed their gratitude for simple things – God's presence while they were milking their cows or laying the hearth fire before retiring for the night (smooring the fire). Their prayers were so simple and expressed such a communion with God that I wondered whether my feeble attempts at prayer, by comparison, were able to reach my Savior.

I learned from the book, <u>How the Irish Saved Civilization</u>, how the early Desert Fathers from Egypt sailed to Ireland to bring Christianity to the area and how they and the Irish monks that followed them had saved Christianity from extinction during the Dark Ages in Europe.

I had always enjoyed Irish music and thought perhaps there was some Irish blood running through my veins, probably co-mingling with the blood of my Viking forbearers. A liking for Irish music was one of the many traits I shared with my sister, Lindy. My favorite hymn is *Be Thou My Vision,* which I hope will be played at my memorial service in years to come. Another Irish favorite of mine is a poem entitled, "Pangur Ban," by a 9th-century Irish monk, who chased words all night like his white cat chased mice.

Perhaps the following "thin place" shouldn't have surprised me, when one day at work I couldn't get warm no matter what I did. I had been teaching that day, and as I sat at my desk after classes, I felt a chill spread through my body. As I shivered and put on a sweater, I remember thinking that maybe I was coming down with something. One rarely gets a chill in Cairo. It was only when I received a call later that evening from my sister, Lindy, in Olympia that I connected these two events – my dad's passing and my inability to get warm. Had I felt the passing of his spirit? Were there tangible ties between him and me that traversed the miles separating us? Was he saying his goodbyes? Due to the time difference between Cairo and the West Coast of the U.S., it was possible I had felt his death. I'll probably never know until I get to Heaven, but no amount of rational thinking will convince me I had not been witness to my father's passing half a world away. Perhaps rather than the Celtic belief that a "thin place" can occur everywhere, my experience could more aptly be described as the "everywhen" of Aboriginal belief, where God and His Spirit transcend time.

A further confirmation strengthened the belief that I had felt Daddy's passing when my mother, my sister, and I looked upon Daddy's inert body as he lay in repose in the funeral hall. I remember thinking, "That's not Daddy. His nose is too angular. It doesn't look like him." It was only upon reflection, however, that I was able to connect what I was seeing with what I was feeling. Daddy's spirit had already passed, and I was merely looking at the empty shell of his body. He was no longer there but was already in Heaven.

I wrote the following eulogy for my father's memorial service in remembrance of my dad.

Daddy

Who was Hans Mattson? He was born Otto Johanson Mattson on September 6, 1918 in Lake Nebagamon, Wisconsin. He was one of nine children. His mother, Amelia, was proud of the fact that all nine of her children were normal. She would often say, "Nine children and not a throwback among them!"

To his mother, Hans was always Hansy. He grew up in backwoods Wisconsin as a farm boy, a child who knew how to trap rabbits and hunt deer out of necessity to put food on the table. Early on, he showed a remarkable mechanical ability and would take everything apart to see how it worked. Hans would relieve Amelia's doubts about seeing their possessions in pieces by saying, "Hansy fix!" He always did.

To his wife, Jeri, Hans was Hans. He was that good-looking young man with the dark, wavy hair that Grandpa Rudy brought home for Jeri to meet. Hans and Jeri courted during the pre-World War II years and got married before he was shipped off to Puerto Rico as an MP in the army. Hans was a loving, faithful husband for 55 years.

To his daughters, Linda and me, he was always Daddy. Not Dad, Father, Pops, or anything else, but Daddy. Daddy taught us a lot of things:

a love of the Great Outdoors, a love of travel, and a good sense of fairness and right from wrong. He had a big heart; he identified with the working man and was always ready to lend a helping hand to someone down on his luck, whether by fixing something or by giving a sack of produce. Daddy was an avid gardener who even went to the extent of pollinating his tomato plants with a Q-tip the year there was a shortage of bees.

Daddy would sing when he was happy. He had a good sense of humor; much of it was ribald in his later years, but his humor was always evident. Daddy was a strict disciplinarian, and in a household of females, Daddy was always right. He kept his promises. When I was around six, I had a nail-biting problem. He said that if I stopped biting my nails, he would give me anything I wanted. I did, and Daddy took me out to dinner and bought me a cowgirl outfit. For dinner as a six-year old, all I wanted was two pieces of toast and French fries. I think I also got chicken that night.

Daddy was happiest out in the woods, sitting by a stream, and fishing or hunting. Deer hunting season was an important time for Daddy. He delayed his hunting trip until after I was born in late November. He announced my arrival by saying, "Well, we have another doe!"

We camped as a family and spent many vacations fishing in Canada. He converted an old school bus into a camper, and we would drive that up to Canada and back. Upon arriving in Oregon, we spent countless weekends driving the back roads and seeing the sights. We saw more of Oregon than most Oregonians.

Daddy was a jack-of-all-trades. He was a carpenter, plumber, electrician, mason, roofer, cabinetmaker, and mechanic. He could make or fix anything, and he did. He felled the trees in Wisconsin for Mother and Daddy's first home. He logged them out with a team of horses and then built the house with the lumber from the trees. It was a cute, snug little house on Laurel Avenue in Eau Claire, Wisconsin.

Daddy was Mr. Mattson to the neighbor kids. They would ring the doorbell and ask if Mr. Mattson could come out and play. He could hit a softball farther than anyone else, and when Mr. Mattson was up to bat, all the kids would back up way out in the outfield.

To his friends and co-workers, he was Otto or Matt. After moving to Oregon, he found work in the shipyards as a welder and ship fitter. He became foreman and was very proud of the ships he helped build. I remember his giving me advice on how to cut out a dress pattern from material I had laid out on the living room floor. He always gave me tips on how to save material because he compared it to cutting out pieces of steel. He couldn't see wasting either fabric or steel. He streamlined one facet of the ship building industry and invented a come-along, for which he received recognition.

To his grandsons, four of them, he was Grandpa. He finally got the sons he always wanted a generation late. We think some of Daddy's mechanical abilities were passed down to his grandsons. Brian and Scott were sorry they couldn't be here, but Brian wrote a poem for Grandpa that Father Bill will read.

Requiem

Stand and watch the sun pass by
Another man interred in sod;
Stand and ask, of all else, why
This man is taken unto God.

Stand and take your answer then;
Stand, and with your earthly loss,
Hear, "He of souls was loved by men,
And now is with the cross."

And if your heart be still afraid,
Take comfort then in this:
He is in heaven, born, remade,
With nothing there to miss.

Brian Anderson

My nickname was Punks, short for pumpkin, perhaps to denote the round Mattson face and chipmunk cheeks that are characteristic of the Mattson clan.

So, Hans Mattson in his life has been Otto Johanson Mattson, Hansy, Hans, Otto, Matt, Mr. Mattson, Grandpa, and Daddy. To me, he will always be just Daddy. Good-bye Daddy from Punks, Lindy, and Jeri.

§

We don't know why we were brought to Egypt, but living there taught us many things. One of the things we took with us when we left

Egypt is a greater awareness of God in our day-to-day lives. We saw this in the lives of the Egyptians we interacted with, in their culture, and in their language. The two most common words in Arabic are insha'Allah (God willing) and il Hamdu il-laah (thanks be to God). We thank God that He still answers prayers, although not in the miraculous ways that we expect. We're still learning to trust in the Lord, to lean not on our own understanding, and in all our ways to acknowledge Him. Thanks Be to God.

§

Thankfully, Tim did not lose his job, and we were able to complete our four years in Cairo. Although the boys wanted to graduate from Cairo American College (CAC), this was not meant to be, and we returned to Virginia, where the boys finished their high school years. Our plan was to enroll our boys in an American high school to prepare them for their transition to college. Brian had two years at Oakton High School and Scott, three years. Despite our best intentions, our plan to acclimate the boys to American culture before they embarked on the transition to college did not turn out as we expected. Both Brian and Scott faced a difficult transition to the U.S., primarily because they themselves had changed by living overseas.

Chapter Three • Washington, D.C.

*I am attached to you and I follow you...*I remember our four years in Washington, D.C. as a busy time. The boys were in high school and involved in several extracurricular activities – Scott in JV Basketball and Brian in drama. Scott was also taking math classes at nearby George Mason University because he had topped out in math at the high school level as a sophomore. Fortunately, we lived close to the school – for the first two years in a rented townhouse on the back side of the school and for the last two years in a townhouse that we purchased across the street from Oakton High School. Our townhouse was so close the boys could roll out of bed and be at school in ten minutes.

We were very fortunate that both Brian and Scott were easy keepers because they never asked for the latest shoes or clothing. We were a one-car family during their high school years, even though we had four drivers in the family. Oakton High School was located in Fairfax County, one of the wealthiest counties in the nation, and the parking lot at the high school reflected this wealth in the kinds of cars the kids drove to school. We knew that as a Foreign Service family we couldn't compete with the Jones,' and we were fortunate that we didn't have to. Our boys had been raised overseas and had seen poverty firsthand, so not having all the material trappings of the American lifestyle didn't matter to them. For this we were grateful to their upbringing overseas.

For two years Tim was in charge of food security for the Horn of Africa within USAID, and he periodically traveled to Africa for his job. He carried a pager on his belt for the inevitable crises, and he worked long hours, often returning home at 7 p.m. His workday started when he arrived at the Vienna Metro station at 5:30 a.m. By 6 he was in his office working.

In the meantime, I had gotten a job as a Library Technician at the Foreign Service Institute (FSI) in Arlington, Virginia. FSI was the training institute for Foreign Service Officers who would be posted overseas, and they could take language classes and other region-specific classes in preparation for their posting. I worked as a Library Technician for 2 ½ years, and although I initially enjoyed the job and the interaction with the students, I became disenchanted with my prospects for the future. My position was converted to a GS8 in the Civil Service, but I soon learned I was stove-piped at the top of that particular classification, and there was nowhere to go from there without a Master's degree in Library

Science. There didn't seem to be any way to move laterally into a GS9 position, which would have placed me at the bottom of the professional classification.

§

One day I arrived home from work to find Scott standing out in front of the house. He had just gotten a phone call from the coroner in Portland, Oregon, who told him that my mother had passed away peacefully in her sleep. A neighbor friend, Wally, who regularly checked up on my mom, had found her curled up on the couch in her pajamas. The coroner said that Mother had in all likelihood had a stroke.

I had never really known what the word keening meant, but as I began to keen after hearing the news, I wrapped my arms around Scott's neck and wept over my mother's death. As I hung onto his frame, I wept over the fact that Scott had been the one to receive the news at age 15. That wasn't right. I should have received the call to shield him from the responsibility of relating the news.

Tim and I quickly made plane reservations to fly back to Portland for the memorial service. We tried to get a bereavement fare from the airlines, but they would only reduce the airfare by $50, so we were forced to make the hard decision of only buying two tickets – one for Tim and one for me. We would have to leave the boys at home in Virginia because we couldn't afford four full-priced air tickets at last-minute prices. Brian was enrolled in the Governor's School, a summer enrichment program for promising high school kids, held in Richmond, Virginia, and we didn't want to interrupt his participation in the program. Scott would have to stay at home with the two cats, but we asked a friend, Naida, who lived nearby to check up on him. Scott at 15 was a responsible kid and could be trusted to take care of himself.

After Mother's memorial service, my sister, Lindy, and I went through our parents' house to prepare for its sale. Tim was charged with bringing the stuff out of the little bedroom and putting it in the middle of the living room floor. I couldn't believe what came out of that tiny closet. My mother had always called my dad a pile it man – pile it here and pile it there, and the huge pile from the little closet was evidence of his expertise in piling. Mother was also fond of relating a story about my dad. One day my parents overheard their garbage man training his new replacement on our garbage route. The experienced man told the newcomer that "This guy Mattson can pack 40-gallons of garbage in a 20- gallon can."

As Lindy and I went through each item, we laughed and cried, reliving old memories. We pored over old postcards Daddy had sent Mother from Canada on his yearly hunting expeditions, and we sifted through old photos of family camping trips. We each formed a pile of things we wanted to keep as memory pieces from Mama and Daddy. Fortunately, Lindy liked new things, and I liked old things. There were a lot of items we'd have to dispose of in a garage sale, as well. There were only two of us left in our family, and we vowed that no material possession would ever come between us as sisters. Our relationship was paramount.

I called Scott to see how he was doing back in Virginia. What he said warmed my heart as only a child can. "I just have one more bathroom to clean, Mom." Scott knew I liked clean bathrooms, and he was trying his hardest to please me and make the situation better.

Our most difficult task was attacking the two-car garage, which was so crammed with tools and every single nut and bolt Daddy ever had that there was barely space to walk single file to the workbench. We enlisted the help of Tim's mom and dad to sort and discard the items from Daddy's garage. We called Goodwill and Salvation Army to pick up items from the house. Toward the end when we could finally see the floor, we paid for six six-yard dumpsters, which we filled with shovelfuls of old and rusty debris. We couldn't believe how much junk Daddy had collected, and we began to understand that Daddy's Alzheimer's had manifested itself 10-15 years earlier in his penchant to collect unusable items in multiples of threes. After a week of work cleaning out the garage, Tim had to leave Portland to return to Virginia, but I requested an additional week to finish going through the house and garage. After our week's exercise of sorting and dumping, Tim and I decided that the moral of the story was to never do the same to our boys.

We held a garage sale and disposed of most of the items neither my sister nor I wanted. The proceeds from the sale totaled $1,200, which my sister agreed to let me keep because I would need to ship my items back to Virginia. I contacted a shipping agent, who gave me an estimate of the cost to ship my keepsakes back home - $1,200. I could hardly believe the synchronicity of it all. Here I had sold the pile of things I didn't want to pay for the pile of things I did want. It was a very tangible lesson to not hold too tightly to the material things of this world.

§

While I was at FSI, the State Department opened up certain positions overseas within the Foreign Service, and Civil Service employees were encouraged to apply for these Limited Career Appointment positions. I was hopeful as I filled out the paperwork and wrote ten essays required for the examination process. Time was limited, and I found myself racing to mail the completed paperwork at the Merrifield Post Office. Going home traffic was bad, and I barely squeaked through the door before the post office closed. I received notice that I had passed the written section, and I was invited to appear for the oral interview.

I had tried becoming a Foreign Service Officer several years earlier in 1988 and had taken the eight-hour written exam. This was before our posting to Pakistan. I remember wondering at that time whether Tim and I could handle a tandem posting with two small boys. Would I be good FSO material? Fortunately, I didn't have to make that decision because my written scores weren't high enough to make the cut-off for the oral interview. Now, I had a second chance 12 years later in 2000.

By this time, I knew our lives were all part of God's greater plan, and our happiness lay in knowing God's will for our lives. We were all part of God's Divine Drama as our Sunday School teacher, Wadi, often said. Was it God's will that I also become a Foreign Service Officer? I didn't yet know, but I decided to let the process play out to its natural conclusion. My repeated prayer was, "Lord if it's your will that I succeed in this interview, make it happen, but if it's not your will, please don't let me make a fool of myself."

That prayer and attitude allowed me to relax during the eight-hour interview and just do my best. After all, there was no pressure on me. If it was meant to be, it would be. I remember feeling like a fly on the wall during the Country Team exercise, where the eight examinees had 45 minutes to digest a one-inch ream of instructions and prepare a presentation to the others in the group. We each had to argue the merits of our proposal, and as a team we could only fund one with the $20,000 given to us in this hypothetical situation. There was an examiner in each of the four corners of the room watching the eight of us as we jockeyed for prominence at the table. It was a fascinating experience in group dynamics.

I felt good about my performance in the exercise, although I had no idea how I stood compared to the other examinees. The day's activities allowed us to become acquainted with each other, and I found one young man in particular whom I thought would make excellent FSO material. At the end of the day, no one in our group made the cut; our official scores in each of the six categories would be mailed to us. My prayer was answered – I didn't pass, but at least I didn't make a fool of myself.

When I finally received notice of my written scores, I was upset. I had missed the passing score of six points by a quarter of a point! That missing ¼ point appeared in the section marked cultural adaptation. How could they mark me down on cultural adaptation if they were not able to ask about my previous overseas experiences and language learning? They didn't know that I'd already lived in Pakistan and Egypt for eight years. All they had to go on for the scoring was what they had observed in those eight hours. The focus for my Master's degree was intercultural communication, and I knew the test I had just taken couldn't possibly assess my ability to adapt to new cultures. The test was ineffective in selecting the right candidates.

I fumed and fretted, and I considered writing a letter to the Examination Board protesting the results, but it wasn't until I talked with a counselor in the Career Center at FSI that I was able to let go of my dreams. His question to me was, "Pam, do you really want to spend a career in the State Department dealing with Type A personalities? Would you be happy doing that?" I had to admit that no, I wouldn't. God knew me better than I did, and my prayer *had* been answered – just not in the way that I could immediately accept.

My disenchantment with FSI continued, and I decided to make a change. There didn't seem to be any room for me within the State Department system, so I left my job at FSI and started looking for another. I ended up at Northern Virginia Community College teaching ESL at the advanced level, which turned out to be excellent preparation for what I was to do in Bangladesh and later, Indonesia. In looking back, I realized that God's hand was in those experiences as well – all in preparation for where he wanted me in the future.

With both of us working full-time and with our boys in high school at a busy stage in their lives, it felt like the four years flew by in a whirlwind of activity. We felt the dislocation of being transported back to the U.S. from a life overseas that had been slower and more satisfying in many ways. Much had changed in our eight-year absence from the States, and we weren't totally prepared for those changes, especially in the area of technology, which for me has always been a challenge. The following article is one that I wrote detailing my frustrations with the fast-paced changes in technology back home.

Mr. Einstein Was Right

The problem occurred when I had to answer the phone. In our eight-year absence from the States, Ma Bell had been deregulated and you now had to buy your phone from a store. My husband, who enjoys bells and whistles of all sorts, came home with two cordless varieties and installed one in the kitchen and one in the bedroom. Now, there's something wrong when you have to consult an owner's manual to answer the phone. I refused to read the manual in the firm belief that if I had to read the manual, there was something wrong with the phone, not me. Besides, it had one of those irritating beeps that wouldn't go away no matter what we did. We tried leaving it off the cradle. We tried leaving it on the cradle. We tried replacing the battery. (We didn't try throwing it against the wall.) Only later did we discover that the set was defective. We brought it back to the store and exchanged it for the no-frills variety with no optional buttons that could go haywire.

I have an inherent distrust of machines in their new and improved state, which translated, does not always mean better. Consider our porch light. It seemed simple enough at first. It had a switch that when flipped in the up position, should have turned the light on. No such luck. There were two switches on the light itself, with three positions each. It also had one of those electronic eye things that turned the light on in the presence of someone in its path. We never did figure out which positions the two switches should have been in to work the light, but we did discover you had to be taller than 5'6" to trip the light. It didn't give us much confidence to know that a short burglar could burgle away with impunity at our house.

Albert Einstein once said, "It has become appallingly obvious that our technology has exceeded our humanity." I tend to agree with Mr. Einstein. One of the more noticeable technological changes on returning to the U.S. was that you could no longer talk to an honest-to-goodness person when you made a phone call. Instead, you were treated to a litany of menu choices, answering machines, and voice mail. Pity the poor soul who still has a rotary phone. I tried calling the Public Health office to inquire about getting inoculations needed for our sons' entry into the Fairfax County school system. I suffered through sixteen renditions (count them) of "We are currently experiencing delays in our phone system. If you would like to speak to someone in WIC (what language is that?), press one. If you would like to speak to someone in Spanish, press two. For all other inquiries, please hold and someone will be with you shortly."

We had lived overseas in the developing world for eight years before being posted to Washington, D.C. Overseas we often had to adapt to life as it used to be, sometimes decades ago. Returning to the States was a fast forward into the future, and I felt like I was in a time warp, a 21st century Rip Van Winkle, being dragged kicking and screaming into the computer age. I slowly came to terms with those changes.

I'm neither a technophobe nor a computer geek but fall somewhere in between. Admittedly, the day before I left my job at the U.S. Embassy in Cairo in 1997, I was informed that I had 576 unread e-mails. I had been introduced to the e-mail system when I first reported to work and promptly forgot about it, confident in the knowledge that anyone who wanted to correspond with me would know my dislike of new-fangled communication systems and would contact me using other methods. I neglected to take into consideration the official notices sent to everyone on the State Department system. Needless to say, the computer whizzes were not happy with me as they were the ones who had to delete all those messages. I have since mended my ways.

In fact, after approximately 18 months stateside, I have made peace with the machines in my life...mostly. I recognized that the cultural dissonance I had been experiencing was all part of the reverse culture shock that most, if not all of us, experienced on our return "home." Call it an occupational hazard.

I am progressing. I have made the transition from Windows 95 to Windows NT to Windows ME to Windows XP. We even have caller ID on our phone. Now if only I could figure out how to program our DVD...

§

Despite our busy schedules, we tried to engage in activities that would be enjoyable for everyone in the family. We pored over the offerings at National Geographic, and each one of us would choose a film or concert we would all enjoy.

Since the boys would soon be entering college, we did the college driving tour, taking Brian and Scott to colleges in the Northeast and Southeast. Tim and I continued our interest in antiquing, and we discovered that although the Virginia area had a lot of antiquing opportunities, somehow searching for antiques in the Washington, D.C. area was not as satisfying as our antiquing overseas. The following story is one I wrote comparing our antiquing overseas to our antiquing in the U.S.

Antiquing on Three Continents

My husband and I went antiquing one day last fall, a rainy, overcast day just perfect for the sport of hunting antiques. The experience was most unsatisfactory, although we didn't go away empty-handed.

The antique show was held in the Washington, D.C. area at a local university in their cavernous sports facility, evidenced by the artificial surface underfoot and the basketball hoops overhead marked by signs indicating NO DUNKING. It was a large gathering of vendors and their wares: beautifully carved oak sideboards; glistening, fluted wine glasses; and pressed table linens from grandmother's era. What the antique show didn't have and what accounted for our dissatisfaction, were all the elements of antiquing on other continents: musty, incense-filled shops lorded over by proprietors with expansive bellies and the anticipation of finding a treasure among the trash.

Antiquing if properly done, should include mint tea served in steaming glasses that have to be held at fingertip as in Cairo's bazaar, the Khan el Khalili, which dates from the 1500s. It should involve inquiries of your health and the general state of business as well as viewing treasures and workmanship like no other. Antiquing in Cairo involves speaking enough Arabic to indicate to the vendor that you're a resident and not merely a tourist. It also involves being the first customer of the day to buy something, however small, to confer good luck on the proprietor for the remainder of the day.

Antiquing in the Attarine district of Alexandria, Egypt involves winding your way through the convoluted tangle of streets to find the merchant who stocks items other than the gilded, Louis XIV furniture that is so popular among the Egyptians. The Americans dubbed this style Louis Farouk, a cross between Louis XIV and King Farouk, known for his expensive taste and decadent lifestyle reminiscent of the pre-1950s nationalization of Egypt. Perhaps you'll find a geranium-painted tile that can be used as a trivet or a camel-shaped oil lamp.

To end a satisfying day of poking around the antique shops in Alexandria, you must have a fish dinner at the restaurant set up in the street near the Corniche, where you pick your fish from a bucket and watch as the chef prepares it for you on the grill. Afterwards it's good form to toss the leftovers over your shoulder to the street cats that mill around the tables mewing to make their presence known.

Hunting for antiques in Islamabad, Pakistan means threading your way through the dusty treasures in Khawaja's shop on the back side of Melody Market and viewing treasures that originated in Afghanistan, Pakistan, or India. It's listening to the stories behind the dented brass bugle or the stacked tiffin boxes dated 1902, Bombay, stories that remind one of Rudyard Kipling's <u>Kim</u>. It's bargaining for the silver Maria Therese coins, which are dubbed "The Lady with the Big Chest" coins for the portrait of Maria Therese on the obverse. It's buying a copper tray with Kashmiri-carved animals and wondering who the original owner of the tray was and how it found its way to the shop.

Our experiences antiquing in the States pale beside our adventures searching for antiques overseas. Maybe we're not looking in the right spots. We did find a small treasure on our last antique outing, however. It was an old, wicker cat basket that our Pakistani cat, Curious George, has taken ownership of.

§

In many ways our four years in Virginia with Tim working at USAID headquarters in Washington, D.C. was our hardship post. The busyness of life, the struggle to pay the bills and keep up with the cost of living, the growing demand to pay college tuition for our two boys, Tim's trips to Africa to oversee USAID's efforts to combat the famine in the Greater Horn of Africa, and our long commutes to work, all contributed to our desire to return overseas, where life in many ways was much simpler and less expensive.

Brian enrolled for his first year of college at George Mason University, but he dropped out after one extremely difficult semester. George Mason turned out to be the wrong college for Brian, and he returned to live at home, where he floundered for several months until he found a job with a temporary employment agency. Ultimately, he found a job as a pharmacy technician at CVS pharmacy and later at Kaiser Permanente, where he would work for nine years.

Scott enrolled at Duke University, which seemed to be a good school for him. After one semester he, too, floundered and went to a small town in Kansas to live with a friend from Cairo. Scott got a job at K-Mart, which led to his understanding that a job in retail was no life for him. He returned to Duke for another try the next September and again dropped out, primarily due to the differences in the socioeconomics between him and most of his fellow students, who were quite well heeled. Some of those students had parents with private planes who would fly them home for the Thanksgiving and Christmas breaks. We were not as well heeled, and the most we could offer Scott was to pay a portion of his tuition and lodging.

Scott returned home a second time to live with us, and he found a job working nights stocking books at Borders. My trip to North Carolina to pick Scott up from Duke was bitter sweet. We were proud of Scott for trying to make a go of it at Duke, but we felt his pain of having to leave school and come home.

At the time, I was deeply resentful of the fact that every penny I earned teaching ESL at Northern Virginia Community College went directly to Duke University, and I could have simply endorsed my check and sent it onward to Duke. For Christmas that first year, Scott gave me a dragonfly hair barrette made of green beads and gold colored wire he had bought at the Sarah P. Duke garden shop on campus. Over time, I came to view that barrette as my $30,000 barrette for it was the most tangible thing we received for our payments to the school. Now I can laugh about my expensive barrette because Scott returned to school at George Mason University and graduated with Honors with a dual degree in economics and English.

Our boys' educational experiences were a learning process for all of us. When we joined Scott for Parents' Weekend that first fall, we noticed that Scott was not his usual self. He didn't introduce us to any of his friends, nor did he talk much about his classes. We thought perhaps Scott was struggling in his transition to Duke, so we went to the school's counseling office to see if we could get him some help. Ultimately, we found that the only role a parent plays in his child's education is to pay the bills. Students at the age of 18 are considered adults, and the school considers it an invasion of the student's privacy to share information with the parents. We were not allowed to see Scott's grades, nor arrange for a tutor for him. We didn't learn about Scott's failing grades until it was too late for all of us.

It was about this time when both of our boys were struggling that our Pakistani cat, George, died. We had not seen George for a couple of days, but one day we found him curled up under Brian's bed. He was reluctant to come out from under the bed, and he wouldn't eat or drink. That night, George cried out in the middle of the night and we found him in the hallway, where he had peed on the carpet. This was not like George, so Tim, Brian, and I raced him to the emergency vet in Vienna and waited for hours to find out whether he would make it or not. The lady vet said George's liver was not functioning and he likely had either gotten into some anti-freeze or had eaten a mouse that had been poisoned. It didn't look good. The vet told us she would call us if anything happened and we should go home and get some rest. We tearfully said our goodbyes to George and prayed he would recover.

We were scheduled to pick Scott up at Union Station at noon that day because he had taken the train from Durham to D.C. to be home with us for Christmas. We got the call from the vet that morning saying George had passed away from liver failure. Fortunately, we were all able to say our goodbyes to George – even Kaydu, who sniffed George's cold and inert body. I found a Pakistani tablecloth to wrap George's body in, and Tim and Scott dug a hole in our back yard for George's grave.

Some months later, I was talking with my friend, Bev, at NOVA, and I learned there were several teachers who had lost beloved cats that year. Bev had read a book called <u>Stone Cats</u>, written by a Japanese artist who decided to paint rocks to look like cats, and she thought it would be a good idea to honor our own pets with a memorial rock. The only problem was that we were to find our own rock and meet at the Arboretum in D.C., where one of the teachers at NOVA volunteered.

Since it was cold that February day, I didn't know where I would be able to find a cat-shaped rock in the dead of winter. I decided to go to Merrifield Nursery in Fairfax to search for a rock. When I got to Merrifield, I talked to a young man and told him I was looking for a cat-shaped rock to memorialize a pet that had died. He took me out to a distant rock pile and started handing me rocks saying, "Does this one look like a cat?" No, it didn't. He must have thought I was some crazy cat lady as he pulled one rock after another from the rock pile only to have me discard it as not sufficiently catlike.

After 45 minutes in the freezing cold, I gave up the search and walked back toward the main office area. As I glanced at the rock retaining wall to my right, I spied the perfect cat rock! It was flat but nicely shaped, and the best part of all was that it had the imprint of a paw and a tail wrapped around the body, which was in a sleeping position. I asked the young man if I could buy THAT rock in the rock wall. He said he would ask the manager, and he came back with the statement that if I would pay 25 cents per pound, I could have the rock. I was elated!

Bev and I and several other teachers from NOVA met on the following Saturday and painted our rocks. One of the teachers was Iranian, so I asked him to paint the phrase, "Go with God, George," "Huda Hafiz, George" on George's rock in Urdu script, which he did. George was Pakistani, after all, and he was wrapped in a Pakistani shroud, so it was only fitting he should have an Urdu blessing on his memorial stone. We still have George's stone, and it has a prominent place next to our fireplace on the hearth.

§

Brian's college experience the first semester at George Mason University was similar to Scott's in that by the time we discovered he had been skipping classes and not doing his homework, it was too late. Brian came home at Christmas and told us he had dropped out of school. Tim and I could tell by Brian's deeply pained expression that he was struggling to make sense of his college semester. Tears of frustration welled in Brian's eyes as he tried to explain to us what had happened, but I don't think Brian himself understood the series of events, so how could we as his parents understand it?

Would our boys' experiences have been more successful had they spent their entire high-school years overseas at an international school? Tim and I have asked ourselves that question repeatedly. What we do know is that we had no choice of posting after four years in Cairo, and we had to return to the U.S. because of Tim's job. We were physically present in the States when both boys were having difficulties in school, and yet we had no idea how much they were struggling, and we couldn't stop the process from happening.

It was a painful period for all of us, but ultimately, the boys turned their situations around and successfully completed their undergraduate degrees on their own terms. Life has a way of teaching us powerful lessons that work to our benefit. Prayer was a given at the time, and we found the book, Parenting Teens with Love and Logic by Cline and Fay, two Christian psychologists, to be extremely insightful and helpful. That book was a godsend.

In early 2001 Tim learned that our next posting would be Bangladesh, where he would serve as a disaster management and food security officer. Although I was eager to return overseas, I dreaded leaving the boys behind.

Scott at the time was rooming with two friends from high school while attending George Mason and working at Borders. Brian was still living at home, and we encouraged him to find another place to live as we prepared for our next posting. Some friends of ours had asked to rent the house to them so their daughter could be close to Oakton High School. We thought that renting our house would be a good idea, but we didn't want to leave Brian in the lurch. Rents were high in the Virginia area, and it seemed like you couldn't even rent a broom closet for the amount of money Brian was able to apply to his rent. My worst fear was leaving for Bangladesh with Brian standing on the front lawn of our townhouse with all his worldly possessions strewn in front of him.

Our prayers were finally answered when Brian found a basement apartment to rent in Herndon just weeks ahead of our departure for Bangladesh. Saying goodbye to our boys, knowing that it would be at least a year before we saw them again, was one of the hardest things I've ever done.

We didn't know at the time the many struggles both boys would face while we were overseas. It wasn't until 2006 that Brian would finally return to school nine years after he had dropped out of college. This time, he did it on his own terms as a 26-year-old at St. John's College in Annapolis, Maryland. St. John's is the second oldest college in the U.S. after Harvard, and it is known for its Great Books Program, where students study the original writings of philosophers, theologians, and mathematicians such as Euclid, St. Augustine, Socrates, and Plato. It turned out to be the perfect school curriculum and environment for Brian, and he thrived. Tim and I breathed a sigh of relief as the boys finally found a niche for themselves in the Washington, D.C. and Annapolis areas.

Chapter Four • Bangladesh

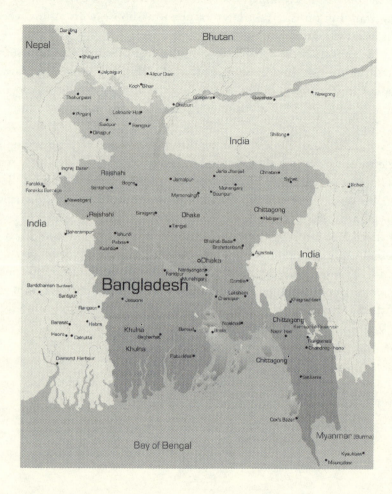

O God, help me to follow you wherever you may lead me... Tim and I arrived in Dhaka, Bangladesh in July 2001 for our next four-year posting. Little did we know that the world would come crashing down in just a few short weeks.

We had recently moved into our apartment in Gulshan 2, a residential neighborhood in Dhaka, when on September 11, the news of the two planes crashing into the Twin Towers of the World Trade Center flashed on the TV screen. My eyes were glued to the news coverage by Katie Couric as I watched replay after replay of the towers collapsing onto the streets below, smoke and debris covering people and cars alike. Two days earlier, news reports had covered the assassination of Ahmad Shah Massoud, an Afghan Mujahideen leader called the Lion of the Panjshir, on September 9, 2001 in Afghanistan. Tim was prescient in connecting these two major events, although I was skeptical of the connection at first. We had no idea how the enormity of the events of September 11 would affect us living overseas in Bangladesh.

Our primary form of communication with friends and family back home was through e-mails, so I sent the following letter to our loved ones to reassure them that Tim and I were safe.

Letter from Bangladesh

September 22, 2001

Dear Family and Friends,

This is a letter to all of you who have kept in close contact with us by e-mail and snail mail and to those of you who may not even know that Tim and I are currently living in Dhaka, Bangladesh.

Like all of you, we have been tremendously saddened by the events of this past week, and we have experienced the emotional roller coaster that such events trigger. We are extremely fortunate that we don't know anyone killed or missing in New York, Pennsylvania, and Washington. We have been glued to the TV (when we receive the signal, but that's another story) and have found it difficult to pull ourselves away. But, life goes on. As I write this, Tim is attending and speaking at an Earthquake Preparedness Conference of Non-Governmental Organizations (NGOs) and development organizations whose job is to prepare for and to mitigate the effects of natural disasters.

How are we doing? We're fine and safe. We're keeping a low profile and trying to maintain a balanced view of life here in Bangladesh as we anticipate what the future holds and how a war in this part of the world may affect us personally as well as how it will affect the larger American community. The American community here has a good communication network, and we have been told to make contingency plans in the event that the situation worsens. We will be taken care of.

We have been encouraged by the AID Director's words that USAID is here for the long run. We are also comforted by the fact that five of the AID families here in Dhaka were also previously evacuated. Quite a few families have had the experience of being evacuated at least once – we have an exceptional USAID staff. Experience helps in knowing what to expect. We are also encouraged by the Bangladeshis' condolences to America and their support in the fight against terrorism. Remember that Bangladesh also lost 50 people in the World Trade Center disaster. By and large, Bangladeshis support us and rally behind us, but their attention is also focused on the upcoming elections scheduled for Oct. 1. Political violence and killings have taken place, but people are hoping for a relatively violence-free democratic election.

This morning we watched the Tribute to Heroes telethon broadcast from Los Angeles. I was brought to tears by the outpouring of love, support, and tolerance expressed in the words and songs of the participants. We truly are a great nation and I was reminded that this was an historical, cultural event that will be long remembered. But I was also chagrined by the images of young Muslim school children who have felt the fear of being targeted simply because they are Muslim.

We, too, as a community have been the target of anti-American demonstrations because of who we are and what we look like. It is difficult to live with those fears. We have been told to stay close to home during two anti-American demonstrations, the first led by Iraqis, 800 persons strong. We have tried to quell our fears upon watching the Taliban's response to President Bush's ultimatum and their call for a holy jihad. Immediately after that broadcast, our cable TV was cut off and remained off until the next morning. After a call to the repair company and being told the cable was down all over Bangladesh, I assumed that it was a political decision by the Bangladeshi government to restrict access to the news media in an attempt to control the public's reaction to the call for jihad. I was mistaken, but it was a reminder to me how easy it is to jump to false conclusions.

What do you do when fear sets in and you feel cut off from contact with the outside world? You call others and you pray. I need to be reminded of a verse in Scripture, which says that we were not given a spirit of timidity and fear. (Sorry, our Concordance didn't make it into the overseas shipment, so I can't quote the verse verbatim). We also found it helpful to keep busy. Tim finished evaluating applications for a new position within his department, and I experimented with my bread machine by trying another recipe. I have had fun with our bread machine and feel almost like a chemist mixing various ingredients in my quest for a perfect loaf. So far I have discovered that the whole wheat setting bakes at too high a temperature, producing a loaf that's almost burnt on one side. This is not tremendously important news, but the puttering keeps me happy and occupied. Our almost three-month settling in period and last week's events have combined to produce inertia, which makes it difficult for me to be productive. I'm not alone in this, I know.

Both Tim and I keep wondering why the Islamic world, especially the religious scholars, have not come out and condemned the Taliban for representing themselves as the defenders of the true Islam. Most Muslims have been horrified to have their religion equated with terrorism. They need to let the western world know that Islam doesn't condone violence but instead, promotes peace. The Muslims we have known in the past and those we know and work with now, are not the people we see depicted in bin Laden's recruiting video. We were relieved to hear President Bush state that the Americans and their allies are not targeting Islam as a religion, nor nations of people, but terrorists and those who harbor them.

We thank you all for your thoughts and prayers and your correspondence with us. Keep 'em coming. So far, the bills and junk mail outnumber the letters, but we remain hopeful. Our e-mail address is...Our mailing address is... We rely mostly on e-mail and snail mail as we have done in the past.

Love, Tim and Pam

§

As the weeks wore on toward Christmas that first year in Bangladesh, we discovered that our mail had trickled to a stop due to the anthrax scares occurring in the Washington, D.C. area. Our mail from the States was also being irradiated, and what little mail we did receive was brittle and singed around the edges from the irradiation. It crumbled in our hands as we took the letter or bill out of its envelope. We received a new credit card with numbers melted into the plastic card itself. Our mail room workers had to be outfitted with hazmat suits in order to process the mail, and it was an eerie sight, seeing them decked out in their space gear suits and helmets equipped with a breathing apparatus. The mail stoppage was new territory for all of us, and it cut off one form of communication with loved ones back home. We came to rely more and more on our electronic connections.

Holidays spent overseas, especially without our children present, were poignant times, and we often reminisced about previous Christmas celebrations, sometimes with and sometimes without family. The following is the Christmas letter I sent to friends and family that year recalling the events of Christmas in Bangladesh as well as prior Christmases in foreign lands.

Merry Christmas from Bangladesh

The view that faces us as we sit on the couch and I stroke our cat, Kaydu's, silky white curls of tummy fur, is one of Christmases past. I'm convinced we're not what we eat, as the popular adage goes, but where we've been. We take the best of each culture or place we've inhabited, discard the rest, and make those experiences a part of ourselves. The Christmas memorabilia gracing our living room here in Bangladesh tells us so.

Representing the farthest reach into my past is a plastic snow globe with its liquid at half-mast, only partially covering a plastic Santa and Mrs. Claus. We still shake it, watch the snow descend, and marvel at the 45-year-old water the globe contains. Sitting next to the snow globe is Menachem, the velvety camel, his furry head topped with a blue skullcap. Tim saw him in a toy shop in downtown D.C. and couldn't resist buying him as an addition to our Christmas treasures. He reminds us of our trip to Israel with our church group from Cairo. It was truly memorable and one of the best things we've ever done as a family.

To the right is another trip down memory lane, a storybook that opens to Christmas pop-up dioramas of Santa and his reindeer visiting the homes of 1950s-era good little boys and girls on Christmas Eve. One year, I fervently hoped and prayed for a stuffed monkey with rubber face, hands, and feet. That year was also the year my eyes were metaphorically opened by Debbie, who was a mature two years older than me. She told me Santa wasn't real, and that presents really came from your mother and dad. I remember tearing into the box holding my monkey, but I don't remember saying, "Thank you, Mama and Daddy." Maybe my memory was enhanced by the telling and retelling of that Christmas as a six-year-old when my parents' bubble was burst with the realization that the Santa myth had been debunked, and they no longer had the joy of playing Santa Claus.

Our eyes travel to the entryway where the Santa quilt hangs. It represents a Christmas project started many years ago in Cairo but just recently finished this year. It hangs in the entryway where we plan to have a revolving quilt display. We hung the Santa quilt in place of The Flight into Egypt appliquéd quilt that was a gift from Father Bill for serving as his tour guide in Egypt. That wall hanging reminds us of many happy excursions down the Street of the Tentmakers to marvel at the fabric artwork made from snippets and scraps of brightly appliquéd cloth. But where oh where could we hang The Flight into Egypt without putting up another hanger and incurring mega-size holes in the concrete walls? The problem was solved with a little bit of ingenuity by tacking it onto the French doors leading to the living room. We couldn't replace Mary, Joseph, and Baby Jesus with a Santa wall hanging, for symbolically, it's too close to reality and to what's happening in our American culture as we commercialize and trivialize Christmas. The Flight into Egypt now occupies a prominent place in our living room for all to see.

Another Cairo memory is of watching the live Nativity sitting cross-legged under the shamiana, a bright tent covering our outdoor church sanctuary. It all seemed so real - the shepherds leading the bleating sheep and the wise men, resplendent in their silk and brocade finery atop recalcitrant camels. The air was crisp, so crisp that we could see our breath as we watched the Nigerians perform one of their catchy Christmas songs. We couldn't understand the lyrics, but the Christmas feeling came across loud and clear. As the wise men swayed to the rhythm, the camels picked up the beat too. Back and forth, back and forth they swayed until the lips of the camel and those of one wise man came together in a camel kiss.

Back again in Bangladesh our visual tour of Christmas memorabilia takes us to a ceramic bowl in the display cabinet containing papier-mache Christmas balls, each painted with a different Santa face: Central Asian Santa eyes, an oriental Fu-Manchu Santa, a Scandinavian Santa with pipe, and a more traditional American Santa. We bought them at Folk Bangladesh for 60 Taka each ($1 — what a deal!) a handicrafts store just down the street that showcases tribal handicrafts from Bangladesh.

The blue and white papier mache girl and boy skaters stand on the same shelf as the ceramic bowl. They were received in a Christmas gift exchange the year we were in grad school in Arizona. The girl no longer winds up to twirl and smooch the boy in a chaste kiss, but their lips remain in a permanent pucker. The girl skater used to revolve to Laura's theme from Doctor Zhivago, but her key was wound too many times and she is now silent.

Our most memorable Christmas souvenir is the infant-sized red and white striped Christmas stocking that Brian was wrapped in as he came home from the hospital. Our Christmas baby turns twenty-one this year. We're going to miss a very important birthday this Christmas, our first ever away from our sons.

Christmas memories are made more special by displaying the artwork our boys have made over the years. A papier-mache stocking topped with cotton batting "fur," battered but still beautiful in our eyes, belongs to Brian. Scott's play-dough dove of peace hangs on the Christmas tree. It's marked Scott, 1992.

Our felt stockings sewn in Malaysia, remind us of a lonely Christmas spent apart from family while we were in the Peace Corps in 1978. The stockings were one of our few reminders of Christmas in a tropical Asian setting. The stockings were gifted to the boys, but we no longer remember which boy has the reindeer and which one has the snowman. We also cherish the audiotape that arrived in Malaysia weeks after Christmas detailing the family Christmas at home – Dad's thin pancakes, Jonathan's toe, which was injured by the lawn mower, and Kare's upcoming marriage. The voices on the tape somehow made us feel not so distant, though still in a foreign land.

It was in another foreign land, Pakistan, where we unpacked our household effects on Christmas Eve that first year in 1989 and discovered our ceramic nativity set, broken in pieces. I dissolved in tears as I un-wrapped pieces of cow horns, bits of broken donkey ears, and shards of angel wings. Fortunately, the Holy Family was intact. Tim came to the rescue with super glue. His efforts are immortalized by a cow's horn glued on backwards, but after many years, this only adds to our nativity set's charm. Dad constructed a rustic manger to hold our nativity set.

Our brass deer from Sadat, the brass man in Islamabad, pulls a Pakistani sleigh carrying a stuffed Garfield, a gift from Scott. Our wicker basket lined with Christmas fabrics, also from Islamabad, and topped with an antlered deer head, now slightly askew, was meant to hold Christmas cards. It holds one, an all-purpose card from the staff at the American club here in Dhaka, wishing us a Merry Christmas, Happy Eid, and a Happy New Year.

The card sits by itself, a reminder that this year will bring no Christmas cards because of Sept. 11 and the mail shutdown due to the anthrax scares.

And then there's the special food at Christmas – Mom's filbert cookies, Dad's thin pancakes, my mom's Norwegian lefse. My dad used to affectionately refer to them as rags. I'm going to try my hand at rags this year using the round griddle and special rolling pin.

Somehow, it's been very important to us here to re-create a bit of home this Christmas season as we celebrate our first Christmas without our boys. What will we remember from this Christmas? We need to keep in mind that Jesus is the reason for the season and that Christmas is still Christmas whether in Kuala Lumpur, Portland, Washington, D.C., Islamabad, Cairo, or Dhaka. Thank you for helping us to remember Christmases past and for celebrating Christmases present and future.

§

Because Tim and I had lived in two other more conservative Islamic countries, I assumed our adaptation to life in Bangladesh on our third overseas posting would be a piece of cake because the Bengali culture was a much less conservative Islamic culture. How wrong I was. I found it difficult to adapt to the relentless heat and humidity that was present year around. It was like living in my own personal sauna.

I remember waiting for someone to pick me up for a ladies' Bible study shortly after we had arrived in Bangladesh. I didn't know Jean at all, so when she said she would pick me up in the car park located under our apartment building, I agreed. I dressed in a long tunic top and slacks and went downstairs to wait for Jean. After ten minutes had passed, I was soaked through with sweat, even though I was merely standing in the shaded car park. I went upstairs to our apartment to change into shalwar kameez and went back down to the car park to wait. Another ten minutes passed, and I was again soaked through with sweat. There was no word from Jean. I trudged back upstairs to change into yet another shalwar kameez and decided that I would wait in the apartment. If Jean wanted to pick me up, she'd have to ring the doorbell because I was going to wait in air-conditioned comfort.

It was not only the heat that was enervating but the crush of people surrounding us at every turn. Bangladesh was the most densely populated country on earth, and I felt unnerved by living among so many people. We found it difficult getting used to Bangladeshis staring at us, and it took us a while to discover that their stares were merely out of curiosity not animosity.

Beggars were a constant, and I agonized over giving or not giving to everyone in need. Noise was also an issue because Dhaka was undergoing a housing boom due to the influx of people from the countryside, and it seemed like every block had an apartment building under construction. The construction noise was ever present, and I had great difficulty sleeping because of it. Unfortunately, I was also experiencing the physical and emotional symptoms of menopause, which exacerbated all the other issues I was dealing with. We worried about our boys back home because their communications with us were infrequent at best. It was my perfect storm.

I'd always been able to write my way through my problems, and my time in Bangladesh was no different from other stressful experiences when I would sit down at the computer in tears and pound the keys until I was able to clear my befuddled brain. The following is an article I wrote about our early years before we had come full circle in the adaptation process.

Bangladesh and Perimenopause with a Cherry on Top

I've always known that the Good Lord has a sense of humor, primarily for His pairing of my husband, who has a hearing loss, and me, for whom noise is an acute irritation. But when I get to heaven, I have a burning question I want to ask: Why when I'm in the throes of perimenopause, did He have to send us to Bangladesh, of all countries?

I tend to think of our experiences here as a banana split of frustrations, albeit a rather rapidly melting one. You start with a banana of heat and humidity, typical of Bangladeshi fruit and weather. Our friend, Suzie, who had lived in Bangladesh for eleven years, forewarned us that contrary to the common belief that there are six seasons in Bangladesh, there are only two: the wet underwear season and the dry underwear season. After completing one calendar year here in Bangladesh, I can attest to the fact that last year we had fifty weeks of wet underwear and two weeks of dry underwear. Add the rivulets of perspiration that accompany hot flashes, and you can see that my natural state is damp. Thanks to the latest disturbing news concerning the negative health effects of Hormone Replacement Therapy, I can no longer trade future cancer risk for present relief from hot flashes, irritability, mood swings, insomnia, crepe paper skin, Swiss cheese bones, and the "fuzzy brain" syndrome.

Add a scoop of corruption for the fact that Bangladesh tops the hit parade at number one for being the most corrupt nation in the world, according to a recent Transparency International survey of worldwide corruption. It's endemic in every level and sector of society, with top government officials particularly well known for their siphoning of funds from the pockets of the people. It's a fact of life here: You pay your baksheesh and you get the service.

Add another scoop of overcrowding and traffic congestion. Look at Bangladesh with a population of 130 million people on land the size of the state of Wisconsin, and you can see that Bangladeshis live cheek-to-jowl and that privacy is a rare commodity in this country of high-population density. You haven't driven until you've driven in Dhaka with its estimated 700,000 rickshaws plus the odd assortment of baby taxis. It gives new meaning to the phrase, rush-hour traffic. It's also impossible to avoid attracting a crowd of curious onlookers when as a foreigner, you are delayed and forced to wait for any period of time, and it's quite unnerving to serve as the local entertainment for men and boys loitering nearby. How do you act nonchalant with your limited Bangla when 200 pairs of eyes are staring at you?

The third scoop on the sundae represents the countless daily frustrations of trying to communicate both locally when your Bangla is basic at best, but also internationally in trying to keep in touch with family and friends back home. Taking care of business long distance is a kick, considering that expatriate families are an anomaly and don't fit the normal configuration of things back home. We have been trying to obtain an international calling card for over a year now, without success. Compound our telephone difficulties with the mail slowdown due to September 11 and the anthrax scares, and you can see how dependent we are on our electronic connections. Thank heavens for e-mail.

Now for the toppings: Drizzle with the ubiquitous construction noise that awakens you two to three times a week in the middle of the night. Even without peering out the window, I have learned to make the auditory distinction between the heavy chink of a cinderblock versus the thud of a brick being unloaded from a delivery truck outside our bedroom. The shouting of the workmen as they go about their nocturnal business adds to the disharmony of the rude awakening.

Next, sprinkle with the frustrations of daily power outages, water shortages, and frequent strikes and work stoppages known locally as hartals, which bring the country and its business to a standstill.

Finally, add a dollop of empty-nest syndrome for being away from our boys for the first time in our lives, feeling the effects of being halfway around the world from them, and missing them terribly. Top with a cherry of guilt for not being there to help them as they encounter the challenges of young adulthood. Ah, guilt, the gift that keeps on giving.

Help me, Lord. My banana split is melting.

§

Our empty nest syndrome weighed heavily on us, and we regretted our not being present for our sons' 21st birthdays. Neither son was a particularly good correspondent, so our e-mails and letters often went unanswered, leaving us wondering what kind of parents were we to abandon our young-adult sons? We couldn't help feeling guilty for leaving our sons and traipsing off to Bangladesh, even though they both were now adults. The following two articles were written for our sons' 21st birthdays, very important birthdays that we were missing. For "The Measure of a Man," the letter I wrote to Brian, I have included only a few of the sayings that we sent to him, for brevity's sake. The sayings themselves were rolled up, like a Chinese fortune without the cookie, and inserted into a Bangladeshi embossed leather box. We thought that Brian could open one saying a day and sample a daily dose on what it meant to be a man.

The Measure of a Man

Dear Brian,

Dad and I deeply regret not being able to share a very important birthday with you, your twenty-first. We searched for something that might commemorate this special occasion but came up empty. You don't need trinkets from Bangladesh, nor do we want to envision your hoots of laughter if we try to send you anything from here. So, at a loss for ideas, we came up with this: words of wisdom from those who have gone before us in their search for what it means to live and to live well. We especially searched for reflections on the measure of a man because we've delighted in watching you grow from a boy into a man. We thought you might appreciate quotes from philosophers and writers; undoubtedly you're more familiar with them than we are.

How well we remember your arrival that first Christmas. As you grew, you stretched us as parents and challenged us in ways that we didn't think were possible. I remember not feeling equal to the task of mothering you and asking of God, "Of all the babies you could have dropped in our laps, why this one?" There was no answer of course, but I came to the conclusion that the only thing I could do was love you. In addition to challenging us, you've provided us with endless moments of joy and mirth; you've become a wonderful young man, one that we're very proud of.

So, with no more ado, you may now open your gift and sample a daily dose of wisdom, which may on your part elicit a chuckle, a wry smile, a nod of affirmation, or even a shoulder shrug of who cares? We've enjoyed pouring through the quotations, selecting those we think you might appreciate. We hope you open these aware that with each one you receive a hug, some motherly and fatherly advice (well-intentioned), and a very big "We love you."

Love,
Mom and Dad

When you do the common things in life in an uncommon way, you will command the attention of the world.

George Washington Carver (1864-1943)

Blessed is the man, who having nothing to say, abstains from giving wordy evidence of the fact.

George Eliot (1819-1880)

All are lunatics, but he who can analyze his delusion is called a philosopher.

Ambrose Bierce (1842-1914)

The true measure of a man is how he treats someone who can do him absolutely no good.

Samuel Johnson (1709-1784)

Many a man's reputation would not know his character if they met on the street.

Elbert Hubbard (1856-1915)

To love oneself is the beginning of a lifelong romance.

Oscar Wilde (1854-1900)

Knowledge speaks, but wisdom listens.
Jimi Hendrix

Education is a progressive discovery of our own ignorance.
Will Durant

§

We also missed Scott's 21ˢᵗ birthday while we were living in Bangladesh, and I wrote this article to commemorate the occasion. It was comforting to me to come across the statement about child rearing by Charles Swindoll and to find the poem we had submitted for Scott's high school graduation. Both the poem and the statement allowed me to realize that God had been there with us all along. Together with that realization came the awareness that wherever our sons might be, God is watching over them. He loves them even more than we do – however impossible that might seem to us.

I Took a Piece of Living Clay

Fall has always seemed like a time of new beginnings for me. Our children go back to school or off to college for the first time. Some of us start new jobs. Some of us make use of the change of seasons to take stock and to implement those personal changes we've been meaning to put into practice.

One of the most important changes we can make concerning our children is to pray for them more and worry about them less. This is a lesson I need to take to heart as much as anyone.

Our youngest son, Scott, is 21 and living and working in the States. He is not a correspondent. He also hates the telephone, so needless to say, we haven't heard from him since we last saw him in May. He recently moved into a new apartment and hasn't given us his telephone number or address. I feel like he's dropped off the face of the earth.

Am I worried? You bet. My worries, however, are tempered by several reminders that I came across recently concerning child rearing and worries. One of these instructions was from Charles Swindoll in his book, <u>The Mystery of God's Will</u>. His reminder to parents is this: "We have two primary jobs as parents: (1) rearing our children carefully and (2) then releasing them completely. Children don't need our constant oversight or advice when they are grown."

Our children are now 22 and 21 years old, and the years of rearing them carefully are long gone. I don't know about you, but I find that the difficulty is in "releasing them completely."

The other reminder came when I was reviewing my Prayers Answered Log from April 2002. This is my entry for April 24: I had been worrying about Scott, and I had sent up a quick prayer today that God would speak to me through His Word. My prayer was answered. The Streams in the Dessert reading for April 24 is "Now faith is being sure of what we hope for and certain of what we do not see." (Hebrews 11:1 NIV) The reading contained an excerpt about a Dr. Payson, who wrote to an elderly mother who was worried and burdened over her son. He wrote to the mother and told her she was worrying too much about her son and that she should take to heart God's commands in Philippians 4:6 and 1 Peter 5:7.

In case I hadn't gotten the message, I went to close my Bible and to turn back some of the dog-eared corners so they wouldn't be permanently damaged. To my surprise, there was another answer to my prayer, the poem that we used to accompany Scott's picture in his yearbook for his high school graduation. The poem goes like this:

> I took a piece of plastic clay
> And idly fashioned it one day.
> And as my fingers pressed it, still
> It moved and yielded to my will.
>
> I came again when days were past;
> The bit of clay was hard at last.
> The form I gave it still it bore,
> And I could fashion it no more.
>
> I took a piece of living clay,
> And gently pressed it day by day,
> And molded with my power and art
> A young child's soft and yielding heart.
>
> I came again when years had gone:
> It was a man I looked upon.
> He still that early impress bore,
> And I could fashion it no more!
>
> Unknown

I get it Lord.

§

One of the issues I continued to struggle with in Bangladesh was begging. Although Bangladesh carried the distinction of having more non-governmental organizations (NGOs) working in-country to alleviate poverty than any other nation, I still felt helpless in knowing what to do about the poverty I was seeing every day. As a westerner, I felt that we had been blessed with so much more than others whom we were seeing on the streets. We saw so much suffering first hand – the crippled man with a deformed hand and arm that was pressed up against our side car window in supplication; the babies with dirty faces and hungry tummies who cried while being held by their mothers; the old woman who sat on the street corner under an umbrella and using a hammer, broke bricks all day long to produce aggregate for the roads. We had been blessed with so many material things. Shouldn't we share from the abundance we had been given?

We had employed Jobeida, our cook bearer and Ali, our driver, but shouldn't we do more to have an impact on the country? When we shopped, we usually paid more than Bangladeshis did, but we considered that higher price our contribution to Bangladeshi society. Could we, should we do more?

The following article details my misgivings about my giving strategy in Bangladesh. Although I later learned more about giving and its historical antecedents in the book, Rambam's Ladder, by Julie Salamon, I still was not able to square my feelings about the imbalance of wealth and my part in the matter.

Hit–And–Miss Giving

I practice what I call premeditated hit-and-run giving. I console myself with the belief that unlike its close cousin, hit-and-run driving, this practice involves no mal intent on my part nor damage to the recipients of the action. My experiences in Bangladesh lately have caused me to wonder otherwise. Am I being helpful or hurtful? The following quotation from Albert Camus leads me to question my intentions and only deepens my quandary: "The evil that is in the world almost always comes of ignorance, and good intentions may do as much harm as malevolence if they lack understanding."

The other day I went to Tamanna Pharmacy here in Dhaka. Before leaving the pharmacy, I extracted four ten-taka notes from my wallet. Outside, I quickly handed the bills to the four beggars who had been waiting for me. Wails of entreaty came from two beggars I had failed to notice. Now my dilemma was whether to tell my driver to leave or to give in to the pleas for additional taka. I chose to drive off, knowing that I could not possibly give to all.

Bangladesh assaults the senses, and it is impossible to remain neutral in this country of high need, so we all develop strategies to cope with the beggars who tap at our windows as we wait in the congested traffic. Forewarned of the pimps and rings of professional beggars, some choose to give only to established charities organized by NGOs, churches, and mosques. Others prefer to give to certain categories of beggars: the old, the children, the disabled, or the mothers with children. Still others do not give to beggars at all and are content with the belief that they are doing what's best. I believe that for those to whom much has been given, much is expected in return, but how does that translate into practical action?

I am no closer to the answer to that question than when we went to our first post, Islamabad, in 1989, and I was still a novice at the art of being a memsahib. My husband and I were at Juma Bazaar when I noticed a woman in a burkha with her hands outstretched. Tim warned me not to react, but my impulse was to reach into my purse. As soon as I had given to the one woman, I was surrounded by six more shrouded women all imploring me to give them money. They were stroking my face and arms, communicating to a foreigner in the only way they knew how. I was taken aback by this sudden physical contact and was immobilized, not by any fear that they would do me harm, but by the strangeness of the encounter. Tim rescued me by shooing them away.

In Egypt, the official governmental response was to have beggars perform some sort of service, however small, which allowed them to retain their dignity. One, an old man who sat cross-legged and sold tissues, never said anything, but he usually gave me a small smile. The day before we left Cairo, I gave him 20 pounds, and I was rewarded with a beautiful smile.

My discomfort with my personal strategy here in Bangladesh stems from a chance encounter with a foreigner whom I'll call Bob. Although he works for a contractor, his major impact on the country comes from meeting people's needs. It's as simple as that. He spends his weekends buying plastic buckets for people to wash with, shoes for the shoeless, and food for the hungry. He has paid for eye and leg operations. Everyone in need knows who Bob is and where he lives. He has managed to counter all my personal roadblocks to giving: I don't speak Bangla, but neither does Bob. I don't want people coming to my home, but Bob doesn't mind. I can't meet everyone's needs, but Bob manages to meet most of the needs of the people who come to him.

So, what are we to do? Do we really accomplish anything by giving ten taka? Can I be like Mother Teresa or like Bob? There are no easy answers, and perhaps I shouldn't expect any in this land of complexities. But I keep looking for them.[6]

§

My previous experiences in Pakistan and Egypt told me that my attitude in any new post would always be more positive, on balance, when I started working outside the home. Because my pattern was to take the first year off from work to focus on learning the language and getting settled in a new post, my interactions with the local population that first year came from my language teacher, our household help, or from merchants. Once I started working, especially when I was teaching ESL to USAID or Embassy employees, my interactions were always more positive, and I felt I learned as much from my students as they learned from me. My experience in Bangladesh held true to my theory.

I was fortunate to be asked by USAID/Bangladesh to set up a business English writing skills course for the 100 or so Bangladeshi employees of USAID. The course was designed to be a practical, job-specific writing course that focused on the process of writing and revision of letters, reports, and official documents. It also served to reinforce grammar skills in the students' writing, and the daily assignments were actual writing tasks the employees were writing for their jobs. I also utilized peer review and revision in helping my students improve their writing. Over a two-year period, the course expanded to include a pronunciation course for the junior-level employees and a technical writing course for the financial management staff. The Foreign Service Nationals (FSNs) were receptive to the courses, and they improved greatly in their writing skills.

I loved working with the FSNs, and I became acquainted with more of those who worked at USAID than Tim did because all of them were

---

[6] First published in the *Foreign Service Journal* November 2003

my students. Tim and I would often talk "shop" at night over dinner, exchanging insights or swapping stories about the FSNs. As an observer but not a direct-hire employee like my husband, I think my work gave me a unique perspective on USAID. I came to the conclusion that the FSN staff was undervalued vis-à-vis their American counterparts. Many of the FSNs had advanced degrees and were experts in their own fields. USAID as an agency was underutilizing and undervaluing this goldmine of expertise.

During my last year in Bangladesh I became the Special Projects Manager for USAID, and I was given three priority areas to focus on: mentoring, training, and online learning. This job proved to be the highlight of my working career, and I was given carte blanche in determining how I was going to implement these three programs. I was able to implement a mentoring program for the American and Bangladeshi staff; to encourage the FSNs to supplement their traditional classroom training with online training programs through USAID in Washington, D.C.; to set up a library of professional development books and materials; and to conduct a training program for the administrative staff. I felt challenged in the position, and I felt valued for my work.

Tim's job within USAID/Bangladesh was as the Food Security and Disaster Management Officer, a long handle, which meant that his job was to manage the on-going food security program and to respond to natural disasters and help mitigate the effects of them. One of Tim's responsibilities, together with his staff of Bangladeshis, was to work with NGOs such as CARE, Save the Children, and World Vision to build cyclone shelters in flood-prone areas so that people could find safe havens from the devastating cyclones, which Bangladesh was so prone to suffer from.

Bangladesh was a delta crisscrossed by three major river systems that emptied into the Bay of Bengal. Normally, the majority of the land area was barely above sea level, and when three major things occurred at the same time as a cyclone, Bangladesh would experience devastating floods and massive loss of life as well as property. The three elements that would need to coincide to create massive flooding were: a high tide in the Bay of Bengal; large amounts of rainfall due to seasonal monsoons or cyclones; and the letting out of water behind dams farther upstream in India and Nepal.

Although we had lived in Pakistan and had experienced monsoons in that country, our experiences there could not compare with the monsoons we witnessed in Bangladesh. Because the land mass of Bangladesh is a low-lying delta, it didn't take a lot of rainfall to inundate the land. We were fortunate to live in Baridhara in a neighborhood in north Dhaka, and our area was usually spared from intense flooding, but other low-lying parts of the city and countryside were not always so fortunate.

One reminder of the severe flooding that had occurred previously in Bangladesh was the markings on the doorpost of the German Club, located next door to our previous apartment building in Gulshan. The first hip-high marking indicated the 1998 flood. The highest marking, at waist level, marked the water level for the 1988 flood. We had remembered hearing about our friends' flood experiences while they were living in a single-family home in Gulshan. They often talked about canoeing from their living room through their front door and into the flooded street.

Although the 2004 flood we experienced was not as bad as previous floods in Bangladesh, to my eyes, it was the most rain I had ever seen in my life. I loved to sit on our screened-in porch on the fourth floor of our building and watch the curtains of rain come pouring down. I had never experienced such massive rainfall before living in Bangladesh. The roar of the wind lashing the trees and the drumming of the rain on the roof were deafening but exhilarating. The jagged flashes of lightening illuminating the night skies and the rolling rumble of thunder were equally impressive. I was in awe of Mother Nature's power and might.

After the rain had stopped and the water had receded a bit, people would venture out to the streets to go about their business. It was not unusual to see a small branch of a tree sticking up through the water in the middle of the street. That stick marked the presence of an open manhole, and you were advised to avoid it. Because of poverty, people had taken to stealing the manhole covers for the metal they contained. The city had great difficulties retaining the covers, so kind-hearted individuals would often put a stick near the hole to warn pedestrians and drivers alike. It was not uncommon to read newspaper reports about pedestrians who had fallen into flooded manholes and drowned. There was one American woman who fell into an open manhole while walking at night; she saved herself with quick thinking by extending her elbows, which prevented her from falling down into the sewer below.

The following article is one I wrote after hearing about Tim's trip to the eastern section of Dhaka in 2004 to deal with the impact of the flooding on the local population.

Story from the Field: Young Mother Gives Birth during Floods

Just imagine giving birth in a makeshift flood shelter amidst 3,000 people in a facility designed for nearly 800. That was the experience of a young mother who gave birth recently, without medical assistance, at a school in Dhaka that sheltered victims of the 2004 floods. She was not alone. There were several other women expecting babies at that time.

Bangladesh recently experienced its most severe flood situation since 1998. Water from three major river systems, the Ganges, the Brahmaputra, and the Meghna and their tributaries swelled past the rivers' danger points, spilling over their banks and inundating approximately 60 percent of Bangladesh's land area. Regionalized flooding in India and Nepal drained into Bangladesh, further exacerbating the situation.

Bangladesh is a low-lying riparian country where the land averages 30 feet above sea level. Although Bangladesh normally experiences some flooding during the annual monsoon season, this year's flooding was particularly severe due to the convergence of two factors: heavy monsoon rains and high levels of floodwater runoff from neighboring India and the Tibetan Plateau. A close eye had to be kept on the Bay of Bengal also as a high tide would have impeded the flow of river waters into the Bay. This flooding affected 30–35 million people in Bangladesh, leaving them homeless and without adequate water, food, and sanitation resources.

USAID provides funding to CARE and other international humanitarian assistance organizations, often the first providers of relief supplies in emergency situations. CARE used part of that funding to open four centers to provide a daily balanced meal to the sheltered people, particularly pregnant and lactating mothers and children.

The Manda School and college where the young mother gave birth is located just east of Dhaka city. The institution itself became a refuge in a sea of contaminated water. Its base was under water, but the upper floors provided the minimum essentials of life to hundreds of families whose lives had been uprooted by the contaminated floodwaters. Water, food and limited supplies were delivered daily to the 3,000 people by boat, replacing rickshaws and motorized vehicles as a means of transport during floods.

One of the two portable water purification units CARE set up in Dhaka provided clean water. The units have the capacity to pump out 9,000 liters of water per hour. CARE employees filled up five liter plastic containers and ferried them to local communities in need. Hopefully these efforts will help prevent outbreaks of disease, so common in the aftermath of floods.[7]

§

Working at USAID proved to be the turning point in my adaptation to Bangladesh, and I valued my friends and colleagues for their input in my acclimation to life in-country. Here is an article I wrote about the adaptation and assimilation process all American expatriates faced in being chameleons in Bangladesh.

A Cultural Chameleon

If you're like most Foreign Service families, you've spent a lifetime traveling and being posted to foreign locales. You've adapted to the cultures and you've learned the languages, becoming fluent in some cases, but in others, learning just enough to get by. If you're like me, you have a smattering of exotic tongues, most learned imperfectly, but like my Taxi Arabic, it's enough to get you from point A to B. You've learned how to play up those linguistic advantages when they're working for you but also how to downplay them when they're clearly a disadvantage. I remember "neglecting" to include information about my language background on a job application, for who in Salem, Oregon would appreciate someone who had studied six languages? To the uninitiated to foreign life, my language background was out of the ordinary, and it clearly meant that I would not stick around in prosaic Salem.

Adaptation and assimilation to our overseas life mean that we become cultural chameleons, ever changing as the situation demands. We take on the sights, sounds, and smells until they no longer seem strange as we try to view them through the eyes of the nationals with whom we live. Have you ever welcomed a visitor to your home in the developing world and noted how overwhelming the deluge of rickshaws, for example, seemed through his eyes? It gives you, the old-timer, fresh insight into just how far you've come in that adaptation process.

As a foreign family, you eat huevos rancheros for breakfast, tabouleh for lunch, and perhaps chicken with Kabuli pulao for dinner; that is, if the commissary or local markets carry those ingredients. You become adept at

---

[7] First published on the USAID/Bangladesh Web site

the what's-for-dinner scavenger hunt through the local markets, and you share your intelligence with other scavengers doing the same. "Hey, Pic 'N Pay has flavored yogurt from Thailand for only 40 Taka. Check it out."

You learn how to slip back into the everyday routine of the States when on home leave, and you quickly recognize the glazed-over stare of your relatives and friends as they grope for words after only five minutes of conversation. They find it difficult to relate to your lifestyle and have no point of reference with which to communicate.

Your children, when they're back in the States, gravitate to other foreigners in making friends, for those children instinctively recognize a certain tolerance and appreciation for differences. Although intercultural communication experts say it's the recognition of differences that eases communication between people of different cultures, I think it's the commonalities that bind us together. Ultimately, it's the finding of those commonalities among us that determines how we will treat others. If we can recognize the humanity in another that allows us to grieve the loss of a child or chuckle with shared delight at something that tickles our collective funny bones, then we'll have come a long way in understanding others and communicating with them. Let's relish the chameleons among us in our Foreign Service life. [8]

§

Because of the crush of traffic in Dhaka proper, which made it horrendously difficult to go anywhere in the city, we usually restricted our movement to a three-neighborhood area near the Embassy: Gulshan, Banani, and Baridhara. Therefore, we jumped at the invitation to explore the Christian cemetery in central Dhaka with Andre and Pierrette, friends and colleagues from work. They were involved as volunteers in the upkeep and renovation of the Christian cemetery in the heart of old Dhaka, and they wanted to introduce us to this part of their lives. Although Bangladesh is primarily Muslim, it has a small Hindu as well as Christian population. We did not know until our visit to the cemetery that Christianity had been introduced to Bangladesh centuries earlier with the arrival of the Armenians in the 1400s. Who knew that Armenians were sea farers and had established a foothold as well as a church in fabled Bengal?

I wrote the following article about our experiences exploring the old cemetery with our friends one rainy Friday morning.

---

[8]   First published in *The Foreign Service Journal* December 2002

Trampling on the Footprints of Angels

I'm usually not given much to reflection or rumination on cemeteries, but I had the opportunity to do just that when I visited Wari Christian Cemetery in Old Dhaka with some friends last weekend.

We departed from home early at six a.m. to beat the heat, the traffic, and perchance the rain. We'd been watching the skies for a break in the monsoon downpours, and we hoped that if not sunshine, at least a lessening of clouds would herald our arrival at the cemetery.

The gray streets reflected the early morning somnolence of a Friday, and the only people we saw stirring as we approached the gates of the cemetery were two Hindu women waiting to enter to pick flowers for their puja.

The heavy metal gates of the cemetery swung open after much pounding to wake the sleeping guard. The barking of the six guard dogs reverberated with the pounding and must have been a rude awakening for the neighbors sleeping in their apartments nearby.

Wari Christian Cemetery covers almost six and a half acres in the heart of Old Dhaka, Bangladesh. It is both hallowed and valuable ground in an area where people live cheek-to-jowl and space is at a premium. What prevails most in this 400-year-old cemetery is the competition between the needs of the living versus the sanctification of the dead. This competition can be seen in the flower-picking women, who have denuded the cemetery grounds of blooms. It can be seen in the space-hungry squatters, who have punched holes through the wall and have built a dwelling in the cemetery, claiming the land as their own. It can be seen by vandals, who have carted away anything of value that is not locked up – gravesite bouquets of flowers and candles and even headstones for the valuable marble they contain. Even Mother Nature has conspired to produce mold and mildew, which carpet the graves, in many cases obscuring the writing on the headstones and leaving the dead in anonymity. Tendrils of creeping vines and trees have taken root among the crumbling stones, giving the effect of graves hidden amid the jungle.

To counter these less-than-benign intrusions into the cemetery, there are a few Christian volunteers who have made valiant efforts to restore the cemetery to a place of beauty and reverence for the dead. They are trying to clear the gravesites of debris and the headstones of mold so that the loving tributes written on them can be read. They are documenting each grave with pictures that have been placed on a Wari Christian Cemetery Web site. They are drumming up support among local and overseas Christians who have loved ones buried in the cemetery. They are trying to resurrect the cemetery as a fitting tribute to all who are buried there.

If only the stones adorning the gravesites could talk! What stories they could tell about the lives that were lived, the likes of Reverend Joseph (last name obscured), the 26-year-old Minister of Calcutta who died in 1724; Herbert Henry Morris, the Indian Civil servant, who was *"killed by a fall from his horse on 3rd January 1868, aged 24;* or Asnat Zia Ghose, a woman with a Muslim given name, married to a man with a Hindu name, and buried in a Christian cemetery. The roster reads like an assembly of the United Nations: J.C. D'Monte, Victor Matthias, Zebulon Daniel, Thomas Anseil (English poet), Diana Catherine Dias, and Lee Chang Wah. One of the youngest to be memorialized is Joshua Aaron Hawkins, who died at the tender age of not quite five years. His headstone reads, *Who plucked this flower? The Master.*

Henry Wadsworth Longfellow, a 19th-century American poet and philosopher said, "He spake well who said that graves are the footprints of angels." If Longfellow was right, we should help those volunteers renew this consecrated ground so that the graves, the footprints of angels, will not be trampled upon. [9]

§

One of our most memorable trips during our four years in Bangladesh was on board a 92-foot traditional sailing ship, the B613. The ship had been named that by the French husband and Bangladeshi wife team who owned Contic Travel in Bangladesh. They were fond of Antoine de St. Exupery's book, The Little Prince, in which the main character lived on an asteroid named B612, so they dubbed their ship the B613.

This couple was trying to save traditional sailing ships in Bangladesh, many of which had been converted to motorized craft with the introduction of the two-stroke engine by the Chinese in the 1970s. During our time in-country from 2001-2005, the balance of sailing vessels to motorized craft had shifted with the traditional sailing boats representing only 30% of all boats in Bangladesh. To educate people about the possible disappearance of traditional sailing vessels, the couple had built several full-size replicas of traditional Bangladeshi boats, which they used in their travel services.

---

[9]   First published on the Wari Christian Cemetery Web site, 2004

Tim and I joined eight other Americans on board the B613 for a six-day journey from Dhaka to the Sundarbans, the largest mangrove swamp in the world, located in southwestern Bangladesh. The B613 was made of teak, and it had a large forward deck with smaller cabins aft that would sleep ten passengers in addition to the crew. The crew of six manned the engine as well as the sails and included a cook, who fed us like royalty. Evenings were spent on the river watching the sun descend below the horizon and listening to the drumming of the tabla, a traditional Bangladeshi drum, by my boss, Jim. Days were spent taking pictures of the remarkable riverine sights we glimpsed from our boat and the bird life that flew overhead. We had hoped to see a tiger on this trip to the Sundarbans, but we were content with sightings of blind river dolphins, gharials, which were South Asian crocodiles, and graceful chital, or spotted deer.

Once we were out of the main shipping channels and away from ferry traffic, the crew hoisted the orange canvas sails, which made our vision of a true sailing vessel complete. Being on the water and listening only to the sounds of the ship's timbers creaking and groaning as she sailed the waters of the delta was such a balm for our harried souls. We had all been working in Dhaka and needed this quiet respite from the hustle and bustle of the city.

The B613 stopped at one of the Sundarbans' forest outposts to pick up a guide for our excursion in the park. We were hoping to catch sight of a Bengal tiger, for which the Sundarbans is famous. I wrote the following article detailing our wonderful memories searching for the elusive Bengal tiger.

Trailing the Tiger in the Sundarbans

"We're on a tiger hunt and we're not afraid." That song of childish bravado is actually about lions, not tigers, but it kept echoing in my head as we trooped through the tall grass of the mangrove swamps of southwest Bangladesh: home to the Bengal tiger.

Well, maybe we were a *little* anxious.

Of course, we were not literally hunting any tigers. Rather, we were on a photographic expedition, hoping to catch sight of them.

Dense forest bordered an expanse of grassland where tigers could easily camouflage themselves and lie in wait for a quick pounce on an unsuspecting deer or tourist. "Oh, that looks like a juicy one, the one with the glasses," I imagined the tiger to be saying to itself as I nervously scanned the jungle just to the right of the path.

Before embarking on our trip, I had read an article detailing the tiger's unique hunting capabilities: "finely adapted stalk-and-ambush hunters, powerful jaws and legendary canines…their striped coloration blends into shadows of forest edge and dry grasses." The article went on to state that each adult tiger needed to consume 6,600 pounds of prey a year. I hoped that we wouldn't be the next meal for one of them.

Our guide, on loan from one of the Sundarbans forest outposts, was nervous and didn't want us to go farther. In addition to being nervous, he had a disconcerting habit of clearing his throat and spitting, a custom obnoxious to Americans but common to many parts of the world, particularly South Asia. I silently referred to him as Mr. Hack 'n' Spit.

Mr. Hack 'n' Spit was unarmed as were the rest of us. Normally, two guides with rifles are assigned to accompany each tourist group. The forest service, however, could spare only one man for our protection. Regulations required that two rangers could carry rifles, but not one, so our one guide came unarmed. Could someone explain the logic of that?

Coincidentally, just that morning, the BBC radio news had reported that only 284 Bengal tigers remain in the mangrove swamps of the Sundarbans, mostly in the Indian portion of the nature preserve. Saving the tiger from extinction seems like a futile endeavor with the loss of their habitat and food sources and with the poaching of the big cats themselves for their supposed medicinal and curative properties.

Selfishly, I suppose, each person in our group hoped to catch a glimpse of a Bengal tiger so he could say that he had seen one in the wild. While waiting and hoping, we were regaled with the bird life of the Sundarbans, both indigenous and migratory: brilliantly colored kingfishers, bee-eaters, elegant, long-necked white egrets, and the stately Brahminy kites, which reeled overhead and seemed at times to escort us. We also saw crocodiles, monkeys, Gangetic dolphins and chital (spotted deer, which some claim to be the most beautiful of the deer family). We even heard the bark of the elusive barking deer, one of the more diminutive deer species.

Although we saw plenty of paw prints and fresh feces, evidence of their presence in the area, the reclusive Bengal tiger eluded us on this trip. Perhaps the tiger is wise to avoid humans, for human contact with this magnificent animal seems only to point to its eventual demise. Again, the line from that childhood song comes to mind, "…and we're not afraid."

We should be afraid... afraid of forever losing one of creation's most regal species, the tiger.[10]

§

Tim and I attended Dhaka International Christian Church (DICC), a non-denominational Protestant church with a membership of 250–300 members representing perhaps 25 nations and as many denominations. The Friday attendance was variable since many of our members lived and worked outside of Dhaka as missionaries, and they only attended when they were in town. The church was housed in the Korean school building on the top floor of the school in Bashundara, and our pastor and his wife hailed from South Africa.

One thing we noticed about DICC as well as other churches we had attended overseas is that there weren't many U.S. Government employees who were church goers. Those who did attend were usually either agricultural specialists with USAID or members of the military, and we wondered what it was about those two jobs that attracted believers. Many of the church's members worked for non-governmental organizations such as World Vision or Save the Children.

DICC was allowed to function as a church, and the pastor and his wife were granted visas as long as the church ministered to the needs of the expatriate population and not the Bangladeshis. As part of the church's outreach efforts, a good friend, Martha, and I put out a quarterly newsletter containing a letter from the Pastor, articles solicited from the congregation, and notices which publicized upcoming church events. Each newsletter had a theme, and the following article is one I wrote for the quarterly issue on prayer.

Prayer Is

Prayer is the fervent whisper of awe that says, "Thank you, Lord." It is the realization that there *is* an all-knowing and ever-present God who loves us and cares for us in remarkable ways. Prayer acknowledges that we can never repay the debt of His sacrifice for our sins.

Prayer is the recognition of our utter helplessness in a desperate situation when we've come to the end of our own resources. At this point, we have

---

[10] First published in *The Foreign Service Journal* September 2002

done all that is humanly possible, so we call out to God in a panicky voice, "Help me, Lord!"

Prayer is the request for divine intervention when the skilled hands of a human healer – a doctor or surgeon – can do no more. Prayer requesting the touch of the Divine Physician acknowledges that we have been fearfully and wonderfully made by our Maker, and only He can right what is wrong and fix what is broken.

Prayer is the wordless gasp of wonderment as we gaze at His remarkable creation, whether it is a breathtaking sunset, a newborn child, or the majestic vista of a boundless sea.

Prayer is the companionable conversation we have with God as we wash the dishes, tinker on our cars, or walk to work. It is thoughts sent on high, confident in the knowledge that God cares about our concerns even though others might think them inconsequential.

Prayer is the comforting words of others, which relieve a burden because it's shared. Prayer can soothe a hurt or calm a fearful heart. Prayer shared is prayer multiplied.

Prayer is the quiet contentment that comes from knowing that we are all part of God's master plan and that our happiness lies in following His will for our lives.

Prayer is.

§

One of our favorite getaways from Dhaka was Nepal, and Kathmandu was only a short one-hour plane ride away. We quickly learned after our arrival in Dhaka that we needed to get away every two to three months to maintain our sanity, and our preferred destination was Kathmandu. In Kathmandu we could experience the cool mountain air I craved after being bathed in Dhaka's year-around sultry, humid climate. We could walk and walk in Kathmandu without anyone following us or staring at us or asking for baksheesh. We could just be ourselves while exploring the delights that Kathmandu had to offer.

We made five trips to Kathmandu during our four years in Dhaka, and we discovered cultural treasures we would return to time and time again. Our favorite hotel was Dwarika's, which had been designated as a World Heritage Site. The hotel compound was constructed of red brick and had been built around the collection of carved Nepali doors and windows Mr. Dwarika had been collecting over the years, some of which dated to the 12th century.

Mr. Dwarika had noticed that beautiful old buildings were being torn down by construction workers to make room for Soviet-style concrete boxes in Kathmandu's efforts to modernize its city. He began to offer the workers new wood in exchange for old doors and windows, and by the time he had amassed his collection, he decided to build a sanctuary showcasing the carving arts of Nepal as well as other Nepali handicrafts. Dwarika's, as the hotel is known, sits at the edge of the city and is a haven of peace within. Dwarika's comes equipped with two resident Lhasa apsos, one of which is named Tenzing after the Sherpa who accompanied Sir Edmund Hillary on his conquest of Everest. The friendly dogs are the hotel's ambassadors, and they sit at your feet as you sip your tea in the courtyard.

Dwarika's has a restaurant that was inaugurated by Prince Charles of England, and if you make reservations 24 hours in advance, you will be presented with a menu detailing the 6, 9, 12, or 16-course meal you have chosen. You sit on the floor with your feet in a recessed area under a table, and you are presented with each course served by a waitress dressed in a costume representing different ethnic groups within Nepal. Each tidbit served is described in your menu. Before you depart from the restaurant, you are presented with a handmade brick that contains an embossed symbol of the Nepali culture. As I sit in my writing studio and type this sentence, I can see from the bricks lined up on the window casing that Tim and I were fortunate to have eaten at Dwarika's on three occasions.

Our favorite room was room 103 on the bottom floor, where the morning sun would stream through the side window and illuminate the window seat where I would sit reading. Outside the room lining the porch would be rows and rows of potted dahlias of every color imaginable; some of them were the large dinner-plate dahlias dressed in pink, yellow, white, and fuchsia. It was at Dwarika's that dahlias became my favorite flower.

We celebrated Christmas 2004 with our friends, Suzie and Jesse, who lived in Kathmandu. We had been staying with them in their home when on Boxing Day, December 26, we heard about the devastating tsunami that had occurred off the coastline of Aceh, Indonesia. The tsunami waves had inundated coastlines throughout SE Asia and even across the Indian Ocean in the Horn of Africa, resulting in unprecedented devastation. As reports of the aftermath were shown on TV and Internet news, Suzie and Jesse became concerned about friends from Nepal who were vacationing in Thailand.

Among Suzie and Jesse's friends were Robin and his family, who were vacationing in the Phuket, Thailand area. Our friends, Suzie and Jesse, couldn't reach their friends by telephone or e-mail to determine whether they were safe, so they decided to fly to Phuket to search for them. They both spoke Thai, having been Peace Corps Volunteers years earlier in Thailand. Tim and I decided to stay on in Nepal but at a hotel so that we wouldn't get in our friends' way. We knew that Tim might be called up to help out in the tsunami relief effort. As reports continued to flow in, we learned that more than 250,000 persons lost their lives in the disaster; Robin was among those who perished. Jesse and Nate, Robin's son, found Robin's body in a mangrove area near the coastline of Phuket.

Tim was called up to help with the relief effort after we returned to Dhaka in January. He went first to Thailand to help with food aid logistics and to coordinate regional and U.S. relief efforts. Later, he was sent to Sri Lanka to assess the situation on the ground in order to determine what was needed by the Sri Lankan survivors. His first-hand experiences in the tsunami relief effort turned out to be extremely helpful in preparing him for his later assignment from 2008-2010 in Aceh, Indonesia, where he would serve as the American Representative to Aceh in Tsunami Reconstruction and Rehabilitation.

§

One of the advantages our Foreign Service life afforded was the close relationships we made when overseas. Usually, there were two strategies that FS families could choose from: you could either try to make friends quickly or you didn't, knowing that you'd only be at post for 2-4 years. Tim and I were in the former category, and we made lifelong friendships we still maintain today. Serving overseas far from extended family meant that your friends became your family. You shared common experiences, which allowed you to speak in a form of shorthand. You didn't have to explain what was going on politically in that part of the world because you all experienced it. Your kids went to the same school, you worked together, you socialized together, you lived in the same neighborhood or apartment building, and you worshiped together. This made for a tightly knit community.

In early 2005 Tim learned that his next posting would be back in Washington, D.C., and although we looked forward to being around our boys again, we knew that Washington, based on our previous history, would most likely be our hardship post again.

111

Chapter Five • Washington, D.C.

*O God, help me to follow you wherever you may lead me...*When we returned to the Washington area, we moved back into our townhouse in Oakton, Virginia near the Vienna Metro station on the Orange Line. It was now home, and we felt we were back in a familiar area.

Tim settled back into his work in the area of food security and disaster management for USAID/Washington, and I set about trying to find a job that would be both financially and emotionally rewarding. I was hopeful that I could continue doing what I had been doing in Bangladesh, only for USAID/Washington. In Bangladesh I had implemented a mentoring program that had been recognized as a best practice. The assessment team that had come out to Dhaka recommended that the mentoring program be implemented in other USAID missions worldwide. I was told to contact the Director of Personnel in Washington to arrange for an interview and to see how my skills could best be utilized there.

Unfortunately, my hopes were not realized. When I appeared at the Director's office, I was shuffled off to someone else because the Director was too busy to meet with me. That person was not impressed in talking with me, and nothing came of that interview. Apparently, I had not made a good impression on him, and he did not recommend I be hired to help implement Washington's mentoring program. I was devastated, and I didn't understand why things had turned out as they did.

I didn't want to return to teaching ESL at NOVA because I had learned that although I enjoyed teaching, my pattern had been to teach for two years until I got burned out and then search for something less taxing on my time and energy. As an introvert, I had to gear up into my teaching mode, and over a period of time this exhausted me. Although I enjoyed the creativity of teaching and interacting with my students, I could not sustain that energy over a long period of time, and I would burn out. I needed a job that was less stressful than teaching. The job that presented itself was as the Office Manager of our church in Oakton, Virginia.

One of the volunteer associate pastors of the church approached me about the position and asked if I would be interested in applying. There were several pluses to the job – I could walk to work, and I knew the people I would be working with. I wouldn't have to invest in a professional wardrobe but could wear what I already had in my closet. This was our home church, and I felt that perhaps God was calling me to the job.

Although I had never been an office manager before, I had had a lot of office experience putting myself through college. I felt that I had the skills for the job, and after the Associate Pastor interviewed me, I was hired.

It didn't take me long to realize there had been a lot of changes that had occurred in the church during our four-year absence in Bangladesh. There had been a split in the congregation when the previous Pastor was asked to leave his position, and now the congregation was half its earlier size. A search for a new pastor had started, but by the time I returned, our church had been without a Senior Pastor for a period of two years. Because of the split, there were a lot of hurt feelings and deep wounds among the members who remained that needed to be healed, wounds I was not aware of. I walked into the position unaware that there had been six Office Managers during the previous five years. Would I be able to make a difference?

The following article is one I wrote after approximately ten months on the job.

Herding Cats and Chasing Rabbits

I'm a cat herder and a rabbit chaser. No, that's not my official job title, but it paints a more accurate picture of what I do than if I were to say I'm the Office Manager of a small Baptist church masquerading as a big church.

I came to the position in the conventional way: I wanted to find a stress-free job in a caring environment. I found the caring environment, as I often tell people by way of explanation for why I work at the church. That and community. I also came seeking community, a rare commodity in the frenetic place that is the Washington, D.C. area.

The cats in my life are the three pastors and countless church members, whom I herd and gently prod into more structured patterns: giving me their weekly schedules; letting the office staff know, in advance, of their needs; and providing the church office with information so that we might communicate to all those who need to know. The rabbits come into play in the myriad details I chase on a daily basis.

"Pam, can you tape these mustard seeds on the bulletin covers? Pam, there's a terrible smell coming from the upstairs hallway, and I need a fresh nose. Pam, I'd like to put an announcement in the bulletin. Pam, the toilets are overflowing in the boys' and girls' bathrooms. Pam, someone's parked in staff parking, and there's no room for the pastors to park. Pam, we need

11 tables in the foyer for the Ministry Fair. Pam, can you get someone on Pew Patrol to put these envelopes in the pew racks for Sunday? Pam, I need some really obnoxious colors of cardstock for the youth."

It's only in dealing with the less mundane requests that I sense a purpose for my being there: Ed's back in the hospital. Shirley has fallen again. Bill is recovering from surgery. A parent is suffering from depression and needs prayer. Carol's cancer treatments have just wiped her out, and she won't be in today. Richard passed away last night at 10:30.

I often ask, "Why me, Lord? Why did you place me here?" Of course, I get no audible answers, but I keep looking for those "on the edge of consciousness" whispers that I sometimes interpret as God's speaking to me.

My perseverance is tested daily, and I chafe in my responsibilities as the official problem solver, the first line of defense when anything goes wrong in the church. Because of budget cuts during the interim period when the church was without a Senior Pastor, we had to make the difficult decision to do without a Building Superintendent for our $8 million church building. Similar cuts in funding were made in the Communications Secretary's position, so by default, I wear three hats and try to take up the slack. I perform triage throughout the day.

My husband and I knew that our posting to Washington, D.C. would be our hardship post when we returned from our four-year stint in Bangladesh. What I remember from our previous posting in Washington was that there was never enough time and never enough money. Who has time to work full-time, take care of family, shop, fight the traffic, cook, clean, and do yard work? Exhaustion would be the word that characterizes my life here in the Washington area.

I had bigger and better plans for my life upon returning to this area, but those were apparently not the Lord's plans. I struggle with my will versus God's will for my life, and I find that however much I plan, God continues to confound me. I guess God doesn't give us a road map of our lives, for perhaps we wouldn't want to go down that particular road if we knew what lay ahead.

While I recognize the fact that God doesn't let me in on His plans, I also believe that whatever happens in response to my earnest prayers for guidance and direction in decision making can be interpreted as God's answers to my requests. Therefore, I consider it my job to bloom where I'm planted and to figure out how best to serve others where I am. Still I struggle.

To set the tone for the church office and to uplift all who enter, I display a Bible verse for the day, a verse chosen perhaps more for me than for anyone else. When I am weary of my responsibilities, I display the verse, "Come to me, all you who are weary and burdened, and I will give you rest. Take my yoke upon you and learn from me, for I am gentle and humble in heart, and you will find rest for your souls. For my yoke is easy and my burden is light." (Matthew 11:28-30 NIV)

I am a natural-born worry wart, having inherited this trait from my mother. When I start to fret, I post this verse as a reminder to all: "Do not be anxious about anything, but in everything, by prayer and petition, with thanksgiving, present your requests to God. And the peace of God, which transcends all understanding, will guard your hearts and your minds in Christ Jesus." (Philippians 4:6-7 NIV)

This particular verse gives me comfort in knowing that I can call upon the Lord in making difficult decisions: "Whether you turn to the right or to the left, your ears will hear a voice behind you, saying, 'This is the way; walk in it.'" (Isaiah 30:21 NIV)

When I start to get full of myself but doubts creep in, I turn to the nuggets of wisdom contained in Proverbs, "Trust in the Lord with all your heart and lean not on your own understanding; in all your ways acknowledge him, and he will make your paths straight." (Proverbs 3:5-6 NIV)

Perhaps my favorite verse of all when I'm trying to deal with the stickiness that we call life is "For I know the plans I have for you," declares the Lord, "plans to prosper you and not to harm you, plans to give you hope and a future." (Jeremiah 29:11 NIV) Somehow knowing that the Lord is ultimately in charge helps to take the edge off.

Although I seek heavenly wisdom, I'm not above resorting to worldly tactics to get through the day. This week I brought my white, porcelain rabbit into the office to remind me that I need to think more lovingly toward the rabbits I chase. He sits perched on my desk next to my computer, and his crossed forepaws and impishly toothy grin make me chuckle whenever I see him. I'm hoping that this attitude will transfer to the other rabbits in my life!

It's interesting that there's not one mention of cats or rabbits in the Bible, so I do my best in dealing with them without the actual guidebook entries or roadmap that would tell me what to do. I listen for those faint whispers. I continue to do what I'm doing, trusting in the Lord with all my heart, hearing the voices behind me, and presenting my requests to

God with prayer, petition, and thanksgiving. Thank you, Lord, for the animals in my life.

§

Unfortunately, I was unable to make much of a difference in the position, and I was unsuccessful in implementing the changes I felt were needed. As the Office Manager, I was given a lot of responsibility but no authority. I tried to communicate the needs of the office staff to the decision makers, but it seemed like no one was listening.

As the communications hub of the church, I felt that I should have been able to attend meetings that created work for the office staff members. I tried to take care of work left undone by my predecessors, but at some point the tasks became overwhelming because of the backlog. I found that many of the contracts the church had entered into had expired or were unnecessary because the contracts had changed over the years, and I found myself in charge of areas that clearly were not my strong suit: computer troubleshooting and church maintenance for example. I lasted for 14 months before leaving the position.

During this painful process, I learned a lot about forbearance, and I learned more about my frailties as well as the frailties of other human beings; even pastors have their shortcomings. I learned that unrealistic expectations often occur when you work in a church. You expect that the people you interact with will always act in a Christian manner, and when they don't, you are often more devastated than you would have been interacting with non-Christians, of whom you have no preconceived notions. I failed to consider the admonition that church is a hospital for sinners, not a haven for saints. My main objective in leaving the position was to maintain good relations with the congregation and still be able to worship with them. This I was able to do, and I was extremely grateful that the Pastor and other members of the congregation could separate Pam the person from Pam the Office Manager.

The next article was written during a Silent Retreat at our church's retreat center, Lost River, while I was still employed at the church. I had already given my resignation notice, and I was looking for other employment. Tim had learned that his next one-year assignment would be Kabul, Afghanistan. Tim was given an opportunity to travel to Kabul to assess the situation before accepting the assignment in the Alternative Livelihoods Program, which meant that he was supposed to come up with alternative crops and related agricultural options for farmers other than poppy. He decided that I should stay back in Virginia rather than go to post with him due to the unhealthy, dangerous living conditions in Kabul. He didn't want to have to worry about both me and the job.

The Silent Retreat

December 1-3, 2006

The blessing for our Saturday Lauds is this: *"I thank my God every time I remember you...being confident of this, that he who began a good work in you will bring it to completion until the day of Christ Jesus."* (Philippians 1:3, 4, 6 NIV)

This would be a good verse to send to Tim as an encouragement. When he called on Friday from Kabul, Afghanistan, I heard tiredness in his voice, flatness, a lack of spark or enthusiasm, perhaps recognition of the reality of the situation after seeing it firsthand.

As for me, I so needed this Silent Retreat. The drive up with Gladys was prophetic in that the weather modeled our departure from the frenetic cares and tensions of daily life in blustery gusts of wind, which buffeted the car and thrashed leaves at us. We came through the congestion of traffic on I-66 at Gainesville, and lo, the sky brightened and lost its angry clouds and forecast the inner peace and serenity that would envelop us at Lost River. How kind of God to provide a symbol for our transition.

My goal this weekend was to re-read The Joy Diet and to implement it. What surprised me were the tears that came so readily as I started reading the chapter entitled, "Nothing." The sentence in particular that unleashed the floodgates of my tears was, "It is when all our somethings are collapsing that we may finally turn to nothing, and find there everything we need."

As I sat there in the Main Lodge among four or five others who had also stayed back from the Contemplative Walk, I found tears escaping, rolling down my cheeks and causing no little consternation when I couldn't get my shoes on fast enough to escape to the veranda and the crisp air, away from helpful and curious eyes. I hoped I could regain a sense of self-control in the cold bracing air, despite the reality of my watery eyes and drippy nose. It didn't happen. *Maybe if I keep walking and focus on the brown, brittle leaves crunching under my feet I can restrain my tears. Maybe if I focus my eyes on the moss and lichen that grow at the base of the bare trees.*

I walked to the covered bridge footpath to watch the water dance over the rocks and to again marvel at the stream, which must be forded by car to get to the Main Lodge. Gladys knows a woman who feels that the stream and crossing over it causes her to leave her problems and the worries of the world behind. I feel just the opposite – that the solitude I seek at Lost River thrusts those problems to the forefront, and in my wrestling with God, I am forced to confront them.

In early morning, the covered bridge over the stream is the perfect vantage point from which to view Lost River. From there you can see the sun touching the top third of the nearby hills, the trees taupe-colored etchings against the blue sky. The sun has not yet illuminated the hills in their entirety, so you can still relish the crisp early morning air and the anticipation of the hours to come.

As the tears continued, I became aware that the stopper had been uncorked from the bottle and there would be no holding back. Unlike Aladdin's lamp, however, this bottle would not hold the promise of a genie who would grant me my every wish.

I thought yesterday morning I had dealt very well with the disappointment of not being chosen for the Office of Foreign Disaster Assistance (OFDA) training job. I had had a premonition that this was not meant to be. I was given the grace to respond to the caller in the face of my disappointment. I truly appreciated the interviewer's taking the time to tell me the bad news by phone. It was more comforting to hear his sincere best wishes and the regret in his voice than to receive the bad news for another job about my being "de-mented" from the Artemis Project in the flat, cowardly wording of the e-mail: "I'm sorry to inform you that..." I asked God – what's the purpose of all these disappointments? I so wanted the OFDA job. That disappointment came on the heels of the sobbing, "I've been deceived" disappointment of the Artemis Project, which followed the slowly building, resigned disappointment that my job at the church was not where I was meant to be.

Where am I to go next, Lord? What am I supposed to do? What is your will for my life? Again, the tears well up, and it's all I can do to blink them down, to try to restrain them by gazing outward at the landscape around me. I am propelled to write on the veranda, with gloved hands that wear my mother's tan kid gloves, which are a tad too small. I find comfort in wearing them anyway as it's a very physical link to my mother, who has passed on.

The air is too cold for my head, which is still damp from my shower. Will I ever be free from the vanity that requires that I try to look my best despite the ever-advancing ravages of time? Does everyone else at the Silent Retreat feel the need for a daily shower and shampooed hair?

I move again, this time to the North Lodge's main room hoping I'll be the only one there. No such luck. There are two others, who probably had the same hopes. I wonder if they feel like I'm invading their space.

The tears keep coming. More tear wiping with sodden, mangled tissues dug from my sweater pocket. This morning I had to break the silence by asking Hank for a box of Kleenex. The box appeared at breakfast time, and I'm glad to see others taking the tissues. I'm not the only sappy one here, apparently.

I'm aware that the mid-day prayer will take place at 11:30, in 25 minutes. I'm also aware that as I cry, my nose reddens, my eyelids swell, giving that too-tight appearance, and my eyes puddle up. I hope no one will notice, for when others are too solicitous, and I feel their concern, the tears come even more readily. I recognize intellectually that ready tears are a sign of stress. I know intellectually that if I were to take the Holmes-Rahe Life Change Units test, I would most likely be off the top of the charts. I don't have to take the test, however, because I can feel it. My bones are very vocal in telling me that. My joints ache, not solely because the insurance company was being persnickety in refusing to pay for a refill of my prescription for Celebrex. Apparently they think they know my body better than my doctor and I do. My bones are telling me what my mind and my whole body already know — I am under too much stress compounded with disappointment.

These past few pages represent the watchfulness of my mind, an act of being nonjudgmental of oneself advocated by Martha Beck in her Joy Diet book. These words are by a writer named Sri Nisargadatha Maharaj:

Know yourself to be the changeless witness of the changeful mind. Mind is interested in what happens, while the awareness is interested in the mind itself. The child is after the toy, but the mother watches the child, not the toy.

I join the group for lunch and, to my relief, am able to control the tears so I can be a reader during lunch. *Thank you Lord.* As I try to be mindful of what my body and mind are telling me, I realize I am so tired. I go back to the room I share with Gladys and sleep the sleep of a drugged person. I awake from my two-hour nap and feel relief and the satiated feeling of having slept and cried it all out. I wonder at my capacity for tears and sleep. Experience tells me these are my drugs of choice. And eating, too, but mindfulness requires me to eat less, not more and focus on what is good for me: smaller quantities at more frequent intervals. No sugar, for it primes the pump and only makes me want more.

In the Main Lodge again, I eat almonds from the pocket of my warm, fuchsia sweater. When I dig in my pocket, strands of sweater fuzz accompany the almonds. I transfer the almonds to my right pocket so my left elbow won't accidentally knock the Styrofoam cup another retreat goer has placed on the armrest of my chair. Silence requires accommodation, so I shift my almonds and my own cup.

Companionable silence is what we keep in the Main Lodge, each lost in her own thoughts and prayers. The glowing fire in the massive stone fireplace is a balm for the tired soul. Some sit facing the fireplace, eyes closed.

I feel good about these pages but wonder if they're a harbinger of future efforts. Will my other words be uncorked and unleashed, much as my tears were? Why is it that tears don't demand the correct venue or time but come unbidden, while words are more fickle and elusive, waiting for the muse?

I take another walk to the burbling brook that passes under the covered bridge. I take the long way toward the North Lodge and down past the meadow, where I notice the tin-roofed barn and the angle it is placed in relation to the hills. It reminds me of the red-roofed barn in Nathiagali, Pakistan and the oil picture that Scott, our son, painted in middle school. He was going to throw it away, but we rescued it as a reminder of our time there but also as a treasure Scott had created. Both barns sit slightly askew – not straight on but ¾ view against a backdrop of the hills. This time at the bridge I notice the wall plaque nestled between the planks of the wall. It reads: *"We live by faith, not by sight."* (2 Corinthians 5:7 NIV) It comforts me.

I am content now to read more and write less, perhaps because the pent-up waters behind the dam have been released. The choices are reading, writing, or quilting. I'm so aware that if I choose one, less time can be devoted to the others, as if time were in limited quantity. I need to learn to live in the moment and to savor what I am doing, not wonder if I should be doing something else. If only I could eliminate the word *should* from my vocabulary.

I like this benediction, which was given for the Saturday Compline:

O Lord, support us all the day long, until the shadows lengthen and the evening comes, and the busy world is hushed, and the fever of life is over, and our work is done. Then in thy mercy grant us a safe lodging, and a holy rest, and peace at last. Amen.

Thomas Merton's Prayer of Abandonment is so appropriate to where I am now:

> *My Lord God, I have no idea where I am going. I do not see the road ahead of me. I cannot be certain where it will all end. Nor do I really know myself, and the fact that I think I am following your will does not mean that I am actually doing so. But I believe that the desire to please you does in fact please you. And I hope I have that desire in all that I am doing. I hope that I will never do anything apart from that desire. And I know that if I do this you will lead me by the right road, though I may know nothing about it. Therefore, I will trust you always. Though I may seem to be lost and in the shadow of death, I will not fear, for you are ever with me, and you will not leave me to face my perils alone. Amen.*

Unconsciously, I think I've incorporated some of Martha Beck's recipe for joy, particularly the element of risk, which she states is a must-have ingredient for a joyful life. She remarks that living to avoid fear is more dangerous than a life of risk, and it can never prevent tragedy. In her book, she related the story about Herman Melville, who felt safe on his whaling expeditions despite knowing that the ropes attached to the harpoons could yank him to his death at any time. Melville didn't feel threatened as a whaler because he recognized that death could occur at any time and any place, regardless of our situation.

Maybe we can use this analogy to explain to our families the risks Tim is taking in his decision to go to Afghanistan.

February 2007 – Two Months after the Silent Retreat

My job at the church ended January 12, 2007, and I am taking some time to discern God's will for my life and the direction I should take. I am sleeping nine to ten hours each night to recoup my strength from the stresses of ending a job and from battling a month-long sinus infection, costochondritis, and bronchitis. I'm wondering whether I should focus on international work, writing, teaching, training, or mentoring – or a combination of all of them. I am, however, not terribly worried about finding a job immediately. I'm availing myself of the quiet time I have to do my devotionals and to commune with God. I'm trying to learn the art of prayerful waiting. Most of the devotionals I read deal with waiting.

God is so kind and loving to meet our needs exactly where we happen to be. I'm so glad he brushed aside the veil of uncertainty from my heart and eyes and answered my prayers. I had been wondering if the past year and the struggles I experienced in the job were a result of poor decision making on my part. Did God lead me to the job, or did I grasp at the bird-in-the-hand opportunity? The answer came in the form of yesterday's reading, February first's <u>Streams in the Desert</u>. What is most encouraging is the verse: *"…for this is my doing."* (1 Kings 12:24 NIV)

In reading the entry for February 1, I was again reminded that my job at the church was no accident; God had placed me in my circumstances so I would learn valuable lessons: to become humble when pushed aside; to depend on Him to meet our financial needs; to turn to Him for comfort when my earthly comforters failed me; and to learn that even in sickness, I could wield the powerful weapon of prayer. I had much need of the holy anointing oil to ease the pain of my situation and to learn to see Him in all things.

> *"Today I place a cup of holy oil in your hands. Use it freely, My child. Anoint with it every new circumstance, every word that hurts you, every interruption that makes you impatient, and every weakness you have. The pain will leave as soon as you learn to see Me in all things."*
>
> *Laura A. Barter Snow*

Lord, may that verse, *"…for this is my doing,"* (1 Kings 12:24 NIV) be engraved upon my heart.

§

During the early winter months of 2007, I pondered my next steps, and I thought perhaps it might be a good time to start an import business importing women's jackets from South and Southeast Asia. I had always loved fabrics, colors, and textures, and I had an impressive number of jackets in my personal collection, gleaned from our travels in Thailand, and our postings in Pakistan, Bangladesh, and Egypt. I took a class called, "Starting Your Own Import/Export Business," through Fairfax County Adult and Community Education in preparation for implementing this idea. I also thought it might be a good idea to acquire more knowledge about fabrics and jacket construction, so I set about finding a part-time job in a fabric store, where I was sure I could learn enough about fabrics to start my own business. I had sewn since I was 12, and I had been quilting for years, so I had a good foundation for learning more. I sought the Lord's guidance on my new venture.

I found a job working 24 hours a week at one of the premier fabric shops in the D.C. area. I started work there with high hopes, but ultimately, I lasted all of two days before I had to call it quits. My left ankle pained me so much I could hardly walk. The job required that I stand for eight hours a day on concrete without the benefit of a padded cushion to stand on, which seemed to run counter to OSHA regulations. The fabric store would not allow its employees to sit down if they were not engaged helping customers. I finally had to acknowledge that I couldn't stand any more, both literally and figuratively, and reluctantly quit the job on April 7, 2007. This was four days before Tim left for his one-year assignment in Kabul, Afghanistan.

As is usually the case in Foreign Service life, your world starts to wobble when your husband is away for an extended period of time. The following is an article I wrote about the trials I encountered during that year of Tim's absence and the encouragement I received from the following verse: "...*Do not be afraid. Stand firm and you will see the deliverance the Lord will bring you today.*" (Exodus 14:13 NIV) That verse provided blessed assurance when I needed it the most.

Stand Firm

It was April 15, 2007, the night a nor'easter blew into the Washington, D.C. area and wreaked havoc throughout our neighborhood by uprooting trees and downing power lines. As I awoke at 3 a.m. the early morning of April 16 to the shrieking and howling gale-force winds, I couldn't help but think that the storm was an apt metaphor for my life at the moment. I finally drifted off to sleep and woke up as the sun came streaming through the blinds, remembering the dream I had just had. I was on the phone with my mother, who had passed away years earlier. She told me that she loved me, and I awoke feeling cocooned in love.

Later that morning, after surveying the 10-foot section of downed fence blown over by the gusty nor'easter, I screwed up my courage in my best Little-Engine-That-Could voice and said, "I think I can. I think I can. I think I can put the fence back up."

My confidence bubble burst when I found myself fending off tears at the hardware store as I contemplated the bewildering number of brackets in the hundreds of boxes arrayed in a 12-foot area. Then it hit me. My ready tears weren't solely a result of the confusing array of brackets and my two hours of frustration at Home Depot. The dam of pent-up emotions had burst, and I was finally allowing myself to grieve my husband's departure for Afghanistan for a year-long assignment with the U.S. Agency for International Development.

My tears were laced with consternation that, by rights, Tim should have been there to help me navigate the complexities of home repair. With the tears came the realization I was on my own and these feelings were perhaps a harbinger of the year to come. I had been left here in Washington to do battle with insurance companies that denied our dental claims and with doctors' offices that double billed us. Overlaid on my grief, consternation, and frustration was a layer of pain from a swollen, painful ankle that still caused me to hobble nine days after I quit a part-time job requiring me to stand for eight hours at a time.

My job hunting attempts ebbed and flowed, reflecting the vagaries of my spirits and doubts about my employment options. Financial worries plagued me, and it seemed like we were existing on the fumes of a once-healthy bank account. Coloring all these emotions were concerns for my husband's safety in an environment that had seen a dramatic increase of IEDs (improvised explosive devices) and suicide car bombings al-Qaeda style.

Just as my worries about my husband's safety, my health, and our financial situation reached a crescendo, the Holy Spirit directed me to a verse that helped calm my fears and allay my concerns. I began to slowly, tentatively at first, lean on the assurances of the following verse: "...*Do not be afraid. Stand firm and you will see the deliverance the Lord will bring you today.*" (Exodus 14:13 NIV)

As I experienced the Lord's deliverance first-hand, I began to believe in the literal application of the Lord's promises of comfort and protection from my worst fears. I started looking for His deliverance rather than focusing on the anxiety and pain that preceded the deliverance. Recognizing my human and fickle nature, I started a diary, an Answered Prayers log, to help remind me of the Lord's assurances. Here are a few of my entries the first few months following my husband's departure for Afghanistan. The Lord's deliverance is written in italics.

"*....Do not be afraid. Stand firm...*" The same day that the nor'easter blew our fence down was the day of the Virginia Tech massacre in which a student shot and killed 32 students and faculty and then killed himself. All day long the radio, TV, and Internet repeated the same terrifying stories about the gunman and his shooting rampage. I tried repeatedly to call my nephew, Jonathan, a graduate student at Virginia Tech, and his wife, Angela, to determine whether they were safe, but there was no answer to my calls.

After numerous phone calls, I finally reached my sister-in-law, Borgny in Oregon, who told me that Jonathan and Angela were unhurt. On the same day I had tried to call my nephew, I called the hot tub company, which had improperly reinstalled the fence after installing our hot tub. That call resulted in the company owner offering to personally rebuild the fence blown over by the nor'easter.

"...Do not be afraid. Stand firm..." Our oldest son, Brian, was accepted at St. John's College in Annapolis. The only problem was the St. John's campus didn't have any financial aid to give him, and the tuition was steep. The college officials suggested he transfer his admission to the Santa Fe campus, which still had some money. Brian requested the money be transferred back to Annapolis, where he was hopeful of finding work as a pharmacy technician. Brian needed $20,000 by September.

Brian again started working seven days a week to earn the money for college. Our portion of the tuition was $5,000, which we would undoubtedly have by September.

"...Do not be afraid. Stand firm..." Our youngest son, Scott, had to appear in court on Friday because of an expired car registration. He didn't have the money for an estimated $2,000 in repairs that it would take to bring his car up to compliance (fix his airbag light) to get the registration sticker. Oh Lord, should I close my 401K to help Scott buy another used car to get to work? The financial company indicated I would take a 50% cut for early withdrawal. Still, 50% was better than nothing.

Brian suggested his car repair place to Scott, and they charged only $800 for the repairs. He paid for the repairs with plastic.

"...Do not be afraid. Stand firm..." We're down to $480 to our name, Lord. How are we going to pay the mortgage, and when will my husband's differential kick in?

Tim's differential kicked in April 23, which was apparently a record for USAID. Both Tim and I breathed a sigh of relief.

"...Do not be afraid. Stand firm..." The secondary dental insurance company denied our claims for two crowns totaling $2,700, which we had paid back in February. Our primary dental insurance company paid only $5 on the claim – less than it cost them to deny the claim and write the reimbursement check.

The accountant at the dental office got the necessary pictures and letters from the dentist for a second submission to the insurance company. Our secondary insurance company finally paid 40% of our claim.

"...Do not be afraid. Stand firm..." Oh, Lord, it seems like every single piece of electronic equipment we have is demon-possessed. I can't renew our Norton Internet Security, despite attempting to renew multiple times and despite several e-mails to their technical support. They don't have an 800 number to call. I can't get into our Lafayette account to monitor our finances because their site is down, or is it because of our internet security or lack of one?

I hobbled to Microcenter, where I met a wonderful salesman who said that everyone had the same problems with Norton. Apparently I was not the computer dolt I thought I was. I bought PC-Cillin, uninstalled Norton, and successfully installed PC-Cillin. Several calls to Lafayette brought assurances that their Web site was down. Jack at Lafayette also helped me to change passwords when both Tim and I were locked out of the account.

Our car's side airbag light kept going on, and it worried me that I would have to pay the $2,000 (Scott's estimate for the repair of his airbag light) which I didn't have, to get it fixed. Our registration expired at the end of May.

When I took the car into the dealership for its checkup, the technician indicated there was a sensor in the passenger seat that sensed the weight of any person or item placed in the seat. If the sensor sensed the weight of a child, the airbag would not deploy, which caused the airbag light to register. I had been placing my backpack and crutch on the passenger seat. The dealership only charged me $34 for their work, rather than the $2,000 I had anticipated.

The downstairs TV had a black box obscuring the picture. I fiddled with the three remotes and managed to make matters worse. The end result was simply fuzz. I gave up in frustration.

Apparently the TV had only a certain amount of memory, and when that memory was overloaded, it caused a black box to appear. The solution was to unplug the TV, and it usually righted itself. A brief power outage solved the problem.

"...Do not be afraid. Stand firm..." I had been hobbling around for more than two weeks when I finally got in to see my rheumatologist. She indicated that my ankle problem was not a joint but a bone problem. She suggested I see an orthopedic surgeon. Where was I going to find one?

Some friends gave me the name of a surgeon who also happened to be one of the surgeons for the sports teams, Washington Redskins and D.C. United. You can't get any better than that!

126

"*...Do not be afraid. Stand firm...*" After having had an MRI done on Saturday, I decided to have breakfast at Bob Evans, a restaurant nearby. I hadn't been there for ages. I saw Pete, the board member who had been so unkind to me during a job interview. He didn't recognize me, but I would have recognized his bulldog face anywhere. Should I let this ruin my breakfast?

I decided that there were so many more positives to focus on — good coffee, good service from Ruthie, our favorite waitress, and the opportunity to read the paper. Thank you, Lord, for choices in attitude.

"*...Do not be afraid. Stand firm...*" I called the surgeon's office seeking an appointment, but they didn't have any appointments for a month. I can't wait that long, Lord. I've already been hobbling for over a month now, and I'm concerned about additional damage to my ankle.

I mentioned that my husband was serving in Afghanistan and it had been more than a month since I had injured my ankle. The surgeon agreed to fit me in on Friday, probably because of the recommendations from friends but also because he had a son in Iraq.

"*...Do not be afraid. Stand firm...*" The next week, when I asked our son, Scott, to take me to my favorite restaurant for breakfast, he said he couldn't because he needed to go to Urgent Care. He woke that morning coughing up blood. I watched him drive away and thought the worst. Also, the cat was vomiting all over the rug, and I didn't have the energy to clean it up. I envisioned having to take the cat to the vet. Oh, Lord, I don't know how much more of this I can take.

Scott had bronchitis and was given antibiotics. He slept a lot for the next few days and got a reprieve on a final paper he needed to write in order to graduate from college. The cat had hairballs, which could be eased if only she'd take her medicine. I tried again to give her the hairball medicine. She seemed better.

"*...Do not be afraid. Stand firm...*" The surgeon indicated that three things were going on in my ankle — arthritis, a partial tear in the tendon, and a possible vertical stress fracture of the ankle bone, which would require tricky surgery and inserting pins to keep the bone together. I felt queasy and had to lie down on the examining table. I told the doctor I was the human equivalent of the fainting goats, a breed of goats in Tennessee with a congenital condition that caused them to faint when they were frightened.

It helped to be able to laugh at myself.

"*...Do not be afraid. Stand firm...*" The surgeon put me in a boot that allowed me to walk, but I was supposed to keep off my foot as much as possible. I also couldn't drive our car, which was a manual transmission, requiring me to clutch with my left foot, an impossible task with my boot. How was I supposed to get around? Life went on.

I decided to swap cars with Scott. It would require getting a current inspection and registration, teaching Scott how to drive a stick shift, and installing a roof rack, but all of those things were doable, if time consuming. Besides, we'd feel better about Scott's driving trip out West if he was driving a more roadworthy car.

"...Do not be afraid. Stand firm..." I'd been unable to reach Tim for the prior three days. I'd called repeatedly around noon our time, which was 8:30 at night Afghanistan time, when he was usually in his hooch. Finally I sent an e-mail, and the returned message indicated that he would be out of his office from May 31-June 9. Now my mind started to go into overdrive. Was he on an assessment for the Provincial Reconstruction Team and couldn't tell me where he was? I knew that a military helicopter had been shot down in Helmand province, and Tim had said that their Alternative Livelihoods Program in Helmand would have to be closed for a period of time until the security situation improved. I knew Tim couldn't talk about events in the future for security reasons, and I was fairly certain that the phone line was bugged and our e-mail communications were read – again for security purposes.

Tim finally e-mailed me from London to let me know that he was sent to England to participate in a counter narcotics meeting. He was safe.

"...Do not be afraid. Stand firm..." Father Bill, an old family friend who had visited us twice in Cairo, arrived on Wednesday for a two-week visit. By Thursday both Bill and I knew that our visit had gotten off on the wrong foot (pun intended). I had had high hopes he would help me keep my spirits up and help out in general around the house. We had talked on the phone of his making dinner to relieve me of that chore.

Bill undoubtedly had had high hopes that the trip to D.C. would help him take his mind off *his* worries. He had been diagnosed with congestive heart failure, and he worried about being a burden on his sister, Elcye, who is a good friend of mine. He was also dealing with severe depression over the church and wouldn't have anything to do with organized religion. Bill was inflexible and wouldn't or couldn't eat what the rest of the family ate. Rather than his making dinner for all of us, we were both making parallel dinners. There went my hopes of being off my feet. We talked during dinner, and I brought up the subject of nutrition, knowing that he needed to follow a low-salt diet. I was aware that I needed to follow a low-sugar diet and to eat low on the glycemic index. He didn't believe in the need for nutrition.

Our talk continued on health issues, and I told him that Scott was resistant to disinfecting doorknobs, counters, and other surfaces so the rest of the family wouldn't catch his bronchitis. Since I would need surgery, I certainly didn't want to catch that illness. Bill didn't believe in germs, either. He didn't want to hear anything about health issues because he couldn't handle it. I said that I didn't want him to fix my problems but just listen to me. After all, I expected Bill, a retired priest, to be all priestly and empathetic. Apparently he was fresh out of empathy.

I suggested that the reason we were having these communication problems was the male/female divide as in <u>Men Are from Mars and Women Are from Venus</u>. Bill thought that was a bunch of baloney as well. Bill said he hoped every dinner wouldn't be as depressing as that one. I went and lay down on the couch to elevate my ankle.

Bill wouldn't use the bathroom that he shared with Scott because of Scott's stinky kayaking equipment hanging in the shower. I showed him Brian's bathroom and suggested he use that one. He left his towel in Scott's bathroom and wouldn't go get it, so I gave him another. He said he was not very flexible. I asked Scott to take his gear out of the bathroom and put it in the laundry room. Scott said it wouldn't dry there. I was caught in the middle, and I went upstairs to bed.

I woke Bill the next morning because I knew he wanted to get an early start seeing D.C. He told me he had had angina in the night, and he took a nitro tablet. At the breakfast table, he debated the wisdom of being here so far from home and feeling ill. He thought about curtailing his visit and called his nephew to give him a heads-up. I indicated that we could go to the Urgent Care clinic and get him checked out. I tried to offer help, and he told me to stop being Nurse Pringle. He said he had lived all his life alone and he just needed to internalize things. I gave him my cell phone number and watched him go off to the Metro.

The remainder of the day was very pleasant. The boys and I went to Sweetwater for lunch for a delayed celebration of Scott's graduation and Mother's Day, and I had the halibut, which was excellent. After lunch, Scott was his usual Mr. Sunshine and suggested we go see a movie together. We chose The Valet, a delightful French comedy that caused us to laugh. We so needed a good laugh.

Bill returned from D.C. having had a good day. He dealt with difficult issues by keeping busy, and exploring was his method. I vowed to myself not to be Nurse Pringle and to discuss only happy topics, thereby keeping everyone's spirits up and perpetuating this emotional charade. I would not put any demands on him. I realized that he was probably dealing with as much emotional and physical baggage as I was, or perhaps even more.

Tim called again from Kabul because he was worried about my situation here. He was such a sweetheart to express concern about me, even though he was dealing with horrendous work pressures himself. He was relieved to hear that Bill and I had (without talking about it) both agreed on a do-over. I don't think I'll ever understand the male mind.

"…Do not be afraid. Stand firm…" I'm still standing, Lord. Thank you. My ankle seemed to be stronger and less painful after almost five weeks in the boot. I was purposely trying to keep my spirits up and to think positively. The daily devotionals from Streams in the Desert *seemed to be written expressly for me, and I took great comfort from their encouragement and, sometimes, admonitions to take heart. I was trying to learn how to* be *rather than to* do, *simply because I couldn't do much of anything. In the process, I found serendipities along the way. This time of forced inactivity had allowed me to be dependent upon others, mostly Scott, who had been wonderful in driving me to doctor's appointments and running errands. I was sure that at 25 he didn't really relish schlepping things for his mom, but that was the situation. I went back to the surgeon on Friday, and I hoped he would say I could avoid surgery.*

Scott had enough points from his credit card for a $400 credit at Borders. He returned from Borders with a box load of books, mostly reading copies of hardbacks or first editions that he wanted to keep in mint condition. He and I went through the books one by one, and he explained why he liked each particular book. I marveled at his reading ability. I hadn't read most of the books; some of them I had not even heard of. I recognized the weighty nature of the classics, however, and I was impressed. I hoped Scott could find a job that would give him a future utilizing his language capabilities, perhaps an entry-level job in editing or publishing.

Scott decided that he couldn't afford to take his kayaking trip out West. I thought his decision was partially based on his concern for me, knowing that I was unable to do many things for myself and that he was the relief team.

I was taking a greater interest in the birds in our back yard. There was a mulberry tree behind our property, and the mulberries were ripe. The birds were having a heyday. I felt like the mulberry tree was a rest stop on the birds' flight patterns. The cardinals were especially lovely, and I watched them intently. I also enjoyed the yellow and black finches. The grackles seemed to be the most quarrelsome, but the robins did their fair share of competing also.

One day I saw one nondescript brown bird feed another. The squirrels also shared in the mulberries and used the branches as a highway to get from the mulberry tree to our back deck. One entrepreneurial fellow decapitated an avocado plant that I had just potted. This avocado pit was the first I had ever gotten to sprout, and I had lovingly coaxed it into growth through the winter. I wish I had been there to watch the squirrel as he tried to carry the avocado pit off. He probably thought he had died and gone to squirrel heaven! I was sure that was the biggest nut he had ever seen. Anyway, I couldn't begrudge his ingenuity or resourcefulness, and I hoped he had enough leftovers to last the week. I did have a mess of potting soil to sweep up, however.

I no longer worried about making my time productive, and I found it refreshing to simply do what I wanted to do when I wanted to do it. I was learning how to be a slug. It wasn't that I thought my immobility would last forever, but it was enough just to be kind to myself. I didn't worry about not having a job or even whether I would ever work again. It was simply not on my radar screen at the moment. My criterion for TV watching was whether it was uplifting or informative, which would help me heal, so I was watching comedy shows. It felt good to laugh, and I thought it was helping my foot. I was learning how to live in the moment and trust in God, and I was reminded of this <u>Streams in the Desert</u> reading:

> "Today I place a cup of holy oil in your hands. Use it freely, My child. Anoint with it every new circumstance, every word that hurts you, every interruption that makes you impatient, and every weakness you have. The pain will leave as soon as you learn to see Me in all things."
>
> Laura A. Barter Snow

"...Do not be afraid. Stand firm..." I'm still standing, Lord. In looking back over the past year, I could see the irony of the admonition to stand firm, when I could barely hobble. It seemed that the Good Lord did indeed have a sense of humor! However, I could also see the Lord's deliverance and how my faith had grown, much like the physical growth of an adolescent.

I remembered comforting our youngest son, Scott at age 11, as he cried out in the middle of the night with growing pains. His leg bones were growing so fast that his ligaments and tendons couldn't accommodate the bone growth. He grew six inches that year and several shoe sizes.

How many inches had I grown spiritually that year, Lord? Like my son's physical growth, my spiritual growth seemed to have progressed in spits and spurts. Occasionally the pain caused me to grimace and cry out, but more often than not, it felt like I was being caressed by the Holy Spirit's presence, whisper-light in its touch. It transformed me, and I marveled at the Lord's deliverance.

My husband completed his year in Kabul and returned from Afghanistan two weeks after the last entry in my Prayers Answered diary. Our youngest son graduated from university, and our oldest son was back in school following his bliss after a nine-year hiatus. Our finances were on an even keel. I had had surgery, four months in a boot, but I was now walking again. For all the many ways that we had been blessed and our prayers answered, I thank God.

§

Tim learned that his next posting would be Aceh, Indonesia, where he would work in tsunami reconstruction and rehabilitation. We were excited about this new posting because it seemed like we were coming full circle after having served in Malaysia in the Peace Corps in the late 1970s. The languages in Malaysia and Indonesia were similar, and we hoped that our long-rusty Malay language skills could be revived. Tim requested language training for his new post, and the agency granted us seven weeks of training in Jogjakarta, the cultural capital of Java. Tim knew that as the American Representative to the Aceh Government, he would need to converse mainly in Bahasa Indonesia, and he would need all the language training he could get.

Instead of renting out our townhouse, we decided to have Scott live there and take care of our cat, Kaydu. She was getting older, and we didn't want her to go through the disruption of the long flights and adjusting to yet another home. We knew that cats didn't adapt very well and that they were most comfortable in familiar surroundings. This arrangement worked out well for Scott also because he was working and by living at home, he could save some money for when he would need to rent his own place. Scott would look after both our cat and our home while we were away. Our townhouse was also fairly close to the put-in on the Potomac River, where Scott frequently went to kayak after work. The situation worked for all of us.

Chapter Six •Indonesia

*I am attached to you and I follow you...*Tim and I arrived in Jakarta, Indonesia mid-June 2008. USAID had made some changes in its office in Aceh, and now instead of both of us working and living in Aceh, Tim would be posted to Aceh and I would be in Jakarta, where the security situation was more stable for dependents. Although we didn't like being separated for yet another assignment, there seemed to be little we could do. The powers that be had spoken.

We took language classes at Wisma Bahasa in Jogjakarta for a period of seven weeks. Because there were only two of us in the class, the language instructors were able to tailor the vocabulary to Tim's needs and provide him with words he could use in his interactions with his Acehnese government counterparts. Surprisingly, our language training 35 years prior when we had served in the Peace Corps in Malaysia came back to us, and it gave us a foundation upon which to build our current language training.

One of our most memorable experiences while in Jogjakarta was visiting the spice factory that a colleague whom Tim would be working with in Aceh, owned. Sam was an American who had lived in Indonesia for more than 30 years. He had married a woman from Sumatra and now had a family of three daughters, who attended the international school in Jogjakarta. Sam also owned a furniture factory that exported furniture to the West and helped manage a coffee plantation in the highlands of Sumatra, from where he supplied coffee to Starbucks.

When Sam asked if we'd like to see his spice factory near Jogjakarta, we jumped at the chance. Sam had bought an old plantation formerly owned by Dutch planters in the 1800s. During WWII, the Japanese had requisitioned the plantation from the Dutch owners and had converted it to an internment camp for Allied prisoners of war. Sam had bought the now derelict factory warehouses and surrounding land for his spice factory, and with upgrades as well as a lot of hard work, he had turned the factory and warehouse area into a modern, state-of-the-art spice processing facility. He employed local Indonesians in both the factory and office areas to help run the facility.

As we toured the immense warehouses and extensive grounds, Sam told us the history of the factory and the ghosts that inhabited the place. As a rational American, at first Sam didn't believe the stories his staff recounted, but over time and by virtue of his experiences, Sam became a believer. Because of his long time in Indonesia, Sam knew that the Javanese people still retained a mixture of animist, Hindu, and Islamic beliefs, and Jogjakarta was the center for the practice of animism. The locals would often engage the services of a shaman to exorcise spirits from an area where they interfered with human endeavors.

While Sam was renovating a warehouse that had once been a barn, he encountered difficulties in sealing the floor. Nothing he applied to the floor would dry – not paint or shellac or any other substance he usually used in his floor-refinishing process. Finally, one of his employees suggested that the floor would never dry because the horses' spirits were not happy with Sam's activities and those spirits needed to be appeased. Couldn't Sam sense that the horses were unhappy? A shaman was called in to perform the appropriate rituals and to repeat certain incantations, after which he declared that the horses' spirits had been appeased. Sam's floor finishing process could continue. Whatever the shaman did, the horses' spirits were appeased and the floor dried.

Another example of belief in the spirit world also occurred on Sam's property, but this time it involved a team of auditors from a major U.S. Fortune 500 company who had come out from the U.S. to audit Sam's spice business. Sam had set the auditors up in the old plantation house, where they could work undisturbed. They were working there late one night when all three of the auditors saw an apparition of what looked like an old Dutch woman in a white nightdress with long hair down her back. She looked at them but didn't say anything. She definitely was from a previous age. The three auditors were so spooked by seeing her that they ran out of the old plantation house and refused to continue working there.

After hearing these stories and having them corroborated by Sam's Indonesian office manager, Tim and I acknowledged that spirits exist, despite our rational American thinking that says otherwise. Although we didn't see the apparition ourselves, we believed in Sam's veracity in relating these stories. After all, we were living in Jogjakarta not too far from the base of the volcano called Mt. Merapi, which periodically emitted puffs of smoke we could see from our favorite coffee shop in town, Black Canyon Coffee. We would sit by the large glass window while sipping our coffee and look out over the rooftops to Mt. Merapi in the distance. Occasionally, we would feel the tremors of small earthquakes and watch as the ceiling lights swayed and our coffee cups rattled on the table in front of us. The 17,000 islands of Indonesia made up part of the Ring of Fire in the Pacific region, a backbone of volcanic activity. We also knew from reading a *National Geographic* article that an old Javanese shaman lived at the foothills of Mt. Merapi, and his job was to periodically appease the mountain's spirits to prevent them from becoming angry and causing the mountain to erupt.

After finishing language training, Tim went to Aceh to begin work. I went to Jakarta, where I started to acclimate myself to living in our apartment on the sixth floor of Executif Menteng Apartments in Menteng, just south of central Jakarta. President Obama had once lived in Menteng as a small child of six, and the Indonesians were very proud of Obama's ties to their country. They called him, anak Menteng, child of Menteng.

I had never lived in a high-rise apartment building before, but our apartment was spacious, and our complex came equipped with a swimming pool, a small café next to the swimming area, and workout facilities. One of the best parts about where I was living was that it was just a short 20-minute taxi ride from the USAID office, which was co-located with the Embassy on the Embassy grounds. As a USAID dependent, I also had access to the Health Unit and the Commissary as well as the APO, all of which were located within the Embassy complex.

We had requested housing close to the Embassy rather than farther south, where the international school was located. Parents who wanted to live close to the school faced a long commute to work, sometimes longer than two hours, especially when it rained and the surrounding area was flooded. Jakarta had literally become a concrete jungle, and the city, which was crisscrossed by a tangle of thoroughfares, highways, and major arteries leading to those thoroughfares, was often unable to accommodate the drenching downpours of rain during the monsoon season. We were amazed at our taxi drivers' ability to avoid flooded areas or traffic tie-ups by taking shortcuts through surrounding neighborhoods to get us to our destination. They called these shortcuts, "jalan tikus," mouse streets.

I was fortunate, again, to be able to work at post, and I set up a business English writing skills program for the Indonesian FSNs that was very similar to the program I had set up in Bangladesh. This time I had 79 Indonesian students, nine of whom were located in Aceh in my husband's office. The nine in Aceh participated in the writing classes via video conferencing. I taught in the main USAID conference room in Jakarta, and my teaching was broadcast live to Aceh. The situation worked well except during periodic storms, especially during the monsoon season, when the high winds and rain interrupted the transmission of signals between Banda Aceh and Jakarta, which were 1,000 miles distant from each other.

I thoroughly enjoyed working with my Indonesian students, whom I found to be intelligent, hard-working and engaging. They delighted in having their picture taken, and they would crowd around smiling and clowning for the camera.

As writing was an important part of the curriculum, I tried to model this behavior and did my own writing while my students were engaged in writing or revising their work-related documents. The following article is one I wrote during one of these writing sessions, and it describes a trip I took to Aceh to assess my students' progress.

Mr. Timothy Long-Stay

My trip to Aceh three weeks ago was part business and part pleasure. I wanted to meet with my writing students and personally hand them their certificates for having completed 16 weeks of business English writing skills. I felt they needed to receive the personalized attention their colleagues receive in Jakarta by virtue of being physically present in the classroom. My students in Aceh participate each week in the writing classes via video conferencing, but they're at a clear disadvantage when I bring treats to class. Watching others eat brownies via remote access is not the same as eating them yourself. So, for this trip next to the certificates of completion, I had packed a batch of rich, gooey brownies – 16 of them, in fact. They represented my last batch of Ghirardelli Square Triple Chocolate

Brownies, which I had saved for this special occasion. My students needed to be spoiled a little, which is all part of a day's work in my job as a writing instructor.

The somewhat guilty pleasure part of the trip was the time spent with my husband, Tim, who lives and works in Aceh, 1,000 miles, four-hours-by-plane, and one transit stop in Medan away from where I live and work in Jakarta. We hadn't planned to be separated once again in this post, but that's what happened. In addition, between the bidding on Aceh and the actual start of work, the job had morphed from having a deputy to help with the workload and living in a communal guest house with all its amenities to having no deputy and living in a hotel. We had hoped that future plans would include our living together in the same location. Still, Tim makes the best of his working and living situation, and we try to snatch some jealously guarded time together. We had been through this before when he was posted to Afghanistan for a year and I was in Virginia recuperating from a broken ankle and surgery. We both know the drill, but still, it's never easy.

This was my second trip to Aceh in ten months, and we were looking forward to taking the long weekend to get away to Sabang, an island an hour's ferry ride north from Banda Aceh, which is located on the very northern tip of the island of Sumatra.

Wednesday night Tim introduced me to his friend, Bart, who is the Advisor to the Governor of Aceh. Tim and Bart have developed a friendship based on shared, vested interests in the sustained development of Aceh, mutual respect for each other's character and talents, a similarly quirky sense of humor, a taste for beer, and a lack of transportation.

It seems incredible that Bart, as the Advisor to the Governor of Aceh, should not have a car and driver at his disposal. Apparently, the costs for a car and driver were not built into his contract, so Bart is forced to bum rides from his counterparts, ride becaks, motorized three-wheel golf-like carts (which are not authorized by the Regional Security Officer), or hoof it. Tim is similarly hamstrung, but he has occasional access to the office-provided car and driver on the weekends. Despite their mutual lack of transportation, their friendship has thrived.

Tim introduced me to Bart Wednesday night at Bart's hotel, The Padi, which in Indonesian means rice growing in the field. Wednesday night is Pasta Night, so we treated ourselves to some of the best-tasting homemade pasta this side of Italy. I had Spaghetti Carbonara with a white sauce that drew out the delicate flavors of the seafood. Go figure. Who knew that

The Padi Hotel in Banda Aceh employed a chef who was a wizard with a saucepan?

Usually, my modus operandi when living in a foreign country is to eat the local specialties. I'd been burned one-too-many times in ordering the falafel in Bangladesh. The actual falafel never quite measured up to the mouth-watering anticipation of it. But maybe that's an impossible task, and the sights, sounds, and smells of eating a fresh-out-of-the-pan, crispy-on-the-outside nugget of chickpeas nestled in a bed of lettuce and bathed with cumin-flavored yogurt, all enclosed in a warm half pita, wrapped in newsprint are not easily found outside the Middle East. But, I digress.

Bart was the one who popularized but did not coin the moniker, Mr. Timothy Long-Stay. Apparently, that's the name the hotel staff have given Tim, and when Bart inquired at the hotel desk for Tim Anderson, the staff responded with "Oh, Mr. Timothy Long-Stay." Tim is one of the few long-term residents at the Oasis Hotel in Banda Aceh.

When Bart first addressed Tim as Mr. Timothy Long-Stay, I thought it was endearing in a Pippi Longstocking sort of way. That's not to say that Tim resembles Pippi Longstocking (other than the red hair), but the two names seem to roll off the tongue with similar ease. I think the nickname has stuck.

Thursday afternoon after work Mr. Timothy Long-Stay and I took the slow car ferry to Sabang. Tickets had not been easy to get because this was Election Day after all, but the timing also coincided with a long, four-day weekend, and hordes of expats as well as locals were getting away for a holiday.

We arrived at the overflow eco-lodge just at dusk, and we found ourselves balancing luggage and gingerly negotiating approximately 80 rough and irregular stone steps down the hill to the lodge restaurant and office – all without benefit of handrails. Only later did we discover that this eco-lodge was designed for the young development set, Peace Corps types, and divers – certainly not for us older, athletically challenged types.

I am still recovering from a misaligned broken ankle and a bum knee, so by the time we groped our way down to the bottom and were told that our bungalow was a third of the way up the hill again in the dark, we decided to skip dinner. Our dinner that night consisted of granola bars and dried figs, washed down with vintage warm water from the malfunctioning water dispenser. It was warm to match the night air, and as we lounged on the balcony, taking turns reclining in the hammock, the tensions of the week subsided. In the semi-dark, the palms lining the beach were silhouetted against the midnight blue evening sky. As accompaniment, we were serenaded to sleep with the soothing slap of the waves on the shore.

The next morning, we took advantage of the cerulean blue water and the opportunities to beach comb and look for shells. Mr. Timothy Long-Stay and I have spent many enjoyable hours, heads down, enjoying the simple pleasures of searching for agates on the Oregon Coast or seashells on the beaches of Thailand. We added to our seashell collection that weekend and even found a book left behind by a former guest, which identified the shells native to Indonesian waters.

Bart and his friend Jonah joined us at the lodge that weekend. Jonah and Bart had forged a friendship when they both worked on their Ph.D. degrees in anthropology at Harvard some 20 years previously. By virtue of Mr. Timothy Long-Stay's friendship with Bart, we were able to share dinner and a very heady conversation with Bart and Jonah. I should also state that in addition to holding a Ph.D. in anthropology, Jonah serves as the Senior Advisor to the Senate Foreign Relations Committee for South and Southeast Asia. Jonah was in Indonesia to participate in a conference on marine environmental issues in advance of the World Oceans Conference, but foremost in his mind that weekend were other more pressing issues in Pakistan: the Taliban's encroachment into sovereign Pakistani territory and the what-ifs of a nuclear-armed country run by a rogue terrorist group.

The topic of the evening was development in Pakistan and the $1.5 billion the Obama Administration wanted to put into the country to counteract the fundamentalist draw of the Taliban. Rarely have I been around movers and shakers, but this was such an occasion. The conversation was mesmerizing, and I was very aware of being a fly on the wall. Time stood still — literally — as I listened to the words being volleyed back and forth among the three men.

While eating dinner, Jonah seized the moment to pick Tim's brain because Tim had served in Pakistan in the good old days from 1989-1993. Would he put $1.5 billion in development funds in Pakistan, and if so, how could the money best be utilized? What would his priorities be? The discussion flew fast and furious, and as it progressed, Tim's responses accelerated to match the tempo. His face took on an earnest intensity, which manifested itself in the rapidity of his speech. Tim was also aware that this might be one of those rare opportunities to bend the ear of a policy shaper, and he wanted to make the most of it.

After we broke away from the conversation and headed back to our bungalow, I discovered that time <u>had</u> stood still. My watch had stopped, but it mysteriously restarted later that evening. Was this a freak occurrence? Something metaphysical? A coincidence? I don't know, but what I do know is that seemingly irrational, not easily explained events have occurred in my life far too frequently to discount serendipity. I no longer believe in coincidence.

The rest of the weekend was spent lazing around walking on the beach, snorkeling, napping, eating, playing Scrabble, engaging in good conversation, and relaxing on our balcony. Perhaps our weekend can best be summed up by a quote from Anne Morrow Lindbergh: "Good conversation is as stimulating as black coffee and just as hard to sleep after."

§

Another story I wrote was one in which I reminisced about all the monkey encounters I had had over the years. We had visited Bali recently, and when we stayed in Ubud, the cultural capital of Bali, I didn't want to visit Monkey Forest, which was renowned for its monkey population on the lam throughout the park. I had had too many monkey encounters by that time, and the following article came out of those recollections.

My Simian "Friends"

It seems ironic that as a six-year-old, the present I coveted and pined over the most was a stuffed toy monkey with rubber hands and feet. I can still picture him in my mind. His face was rubber, like his hands and feet, his eyes amber brown, and his fur a silky carpet, which became matted after all the loving a six-year-old with sticky hands can give.

In looking back, I wonder how my image of monkeys changed from my childhood view to an adult's extreme disliking. Perhaps my early perception of monkeys was colored by a Disneyesque picture of them as cute, playful, and impish – certainly not creatures that could provoke fear in my heart.

My adult opinion of monkeys is an informed one, based on multiple encounters over the last 30 years. Let me tell you about my simian "friends."

My second monkey encounter was in a public park in Penang, Malaysia, where Tim and I went for a brief respite during our time as Peace Corps

Volunteers in Kuala Lumpur. The park was lovely with mature, shade-producing trees and expansive tropical flower beds. What distinguished this park from other parks I had seen was that instead of squirrels scampering freely, this park had monkeys. How cute was that?

I decided to buy a bag of peanuts from the park vendor to see if these monkeys could be hand fed. I held the first peanut out to a nearby monkey, and he took it in his paw and began cracking the shell to get at the peanut inside. So far so good. Now there were two monkeys, the second one hungrily eyeing the first one's peanut. The second one came closer to me and the bag of peanuts and expectantly waited for his peanut, which I gave him.

Gradually as word along the monkey telegraph spread, a small troop of monkeys started to form. First there were five, then ten, then 20, and as they congregated, their chatter increased, and they became increasingly demanding. "I want my peanut, too." they seemed to be saying. When their numbers topped 50, I started to panic. *What if they rushed me and tried to grab the whole bag?* I did not underestimate the intelligence of our close cousins in their ability to extrapolate that if one peanut came from the bag, there must be more of them.

They say when a person feels threatened, there are two common responses: fight or flight. I chose the second, dropped the peanuts on the ground to let the monkeys duke it out, and ran. This second encounter with real, live monkeys did not match the warm, fuzzy memories of my childhood.

My third monkey experience was a vicarious one – through my husband. Tim was on call as the Duty Officer in Cairo, Egypt for that week when he got a call Friday night at 10:00. The voice on the other end of the line was anxious and insistent: "You've got to find the monkey!" At first, Tim thought that this was a prank call, but as he questioned the caller for details, he came to the conclusion that the call was unfortunately legitimate.

As it turned out, the voice on the phone was a man who had been in Cairo attending a conference with his girlfriend. They had been walking along one of the main streets in Cairo when they passed a pet store. The girlfriend couldn't resist putting her finger into the monkey cage. You can guess the rest of the story: the monkey bit her finger, and now the boyfriend was calling from the States to see if Tim could find that particular monkey that had bit his girlfriend in that particular pet store on that particular main street in Cairo. The monkey needed to be tested for any number of diseases that could have been passed to the man's girlfriend.

How quickly could Tim find the monkey? Time was of the essence since the man had already done some legwork in calling the Center for Disease Control in Atlanta, and they had assured him that yes, there were several diseases transmitted to humans with a monkey as the vector.

Of course, the man did not remember the name of the main street they had been walking on, but you know it was one of those main streets near the Embassy. He also didn't remember the name of the pet shop because it was written in Arabic, but the cages were out on the sidewalk. No, he couldn't really describe the monkey, but it was smallish with brown fur. How soon could Tim find the monkey and call the man back?

Tim explained that he was the Duty Officer and this call didn't really constitute an emergency. The man had called at 10:00 on a Friday night, and the Embassy was closed over the weekend. No, Tim couldn't really call out the Marines to help search for the monkey because that wasn't the Marines' job. Tim reassured the man he would do his best the next morning and try to find the monkey.

The next morning, Tim called Motor Pool for the use of an official vehicle with driver (we were new in Cairo and didn't own a car) to cruise the main streets near the Embassy looking for pet stores with monkeys in cages out front. As luck would have it, Tim and the driver did find a pet store not too far from the Embassy, and it did have monkeys in cages out front.

With help in translating from Arabic to English, Tim questioned the shop owner. Yes, he sort of remembered an American woman who was stupid enough to put her finger in the cage. Yes, he thought he still had the monkey, but you know it wasn't really the monkey's fault for having bitten the woman. Why did the monkey need to be tested? Would Tim reimburse the shop owner if anything happened to the monkey?

Tim was fortunate to have found the offending monkey. It was sent to NAMRU (Naval Medical Research Unit) and tested for a number of diseases. Everyone dodged the bullet because after being put through a battery of tests by NAMRU, the monkey came back with a clean bill of health. As for the woman, Tim never heard from her or her boyfriend again. The incident did make for enjoyable reading, however, when Tim had to write it up in the Embassy's Duty Officer's book.

My fourth encounter with a monkey – to be frank, it was a baboon, a very powerfully built creature about three feet high with four-inch teeth

— occurred while picnicking on a bluff above a hippo pool in the Masai Mara in Kenya. Our tented camp had packed a box lunch for the four of us and our driver, and we had stopped briefly on our drive across the game park. As we unpacked our boxes, we all pulled lunch items out of them: sandwiches wrapped in paper, pineapple spears wrapped in plastic, and boxed juices.

All of a sudden, we heard a German-accented, "Watch out!" Before any of us had registered what was happening, the baboon had barreled right into the middle of our picnic, grabbed our youngest son's pineapple spear out of his hand, and started eating it. Startled, I jumped up, threw my lunch in the air, and ran for the van, leaving my husband, our guide, and our two sons to fend off the baboon with rocks. As far as I was concerned, anything with four-inch teeth could have my lunch.

Monkeys, while sometimes cute, can be irritating pests that help themselves to others' belongings. While we were staying at a tented camp, still in the Masai Mara, we were warned to keep our tent tightly zipped and locked so that thieving monkeys couldn't run off with our things. We followed that advice.

We also got a closer look at monkey behavior when it came to food. Meals at the tented camp were set up in an open area under sheltering trees. Guests could sample any number of foods from the long, skirted buffet tables set up in the middle of the clearing. Curiously, the buffet tables had netting draped over them to shield the food from flies, or so I presumed. Not so. From where we were seated, we could see the back side of the buffet tables, and as we watched, furtive, furry brown hands reached up from under the skirted tables to snatch delicacies from under the netting. These monkeys were both sneaky and quick! They must have imagined themselves to be in monkey heaven with such easy pickings.

The tented camp had hired native Kenyans, armed with slingshots, to keep the pesky monkeys away from the guests and the guests' food. Despite the Kenyans' remarkable ability with slingshots, they were poor matches for the nimble monkeys, which merely high-tailed it to the trees if they were caught pilfering food from beneath the buffet tables.

My next encounter with monkeys again occurred in Malaysia, but this time, it happened in Langkawi, islands off the west coast of Malaysia, where we were vacationing one Christmas. We were staying at a resort that had a spa, so Tim and I decided to treat ourselves to an afternoon of self-indulgence. Tim decided to take a sauna while I lazed around the pool sipping fresh lime juice. I was lying on my stomach on a chaise lounge, eyes closed, when I heard that familiar, insistent but cautionary tone, "Madame, Madame," the voice said. This time it was in Italian-accented English.

I opened my eyes, and sitting not more than two feet from my face on the side table was a largish, grey-bearded monkey with his paw in my lime juice. He had the look of a kid who had just gotten caught with his hand in the cookie jar: "Who, me?" I jumped up and ran to the other side of the pool while the pool attendant shooed the monkey back into the forest area that rimmed the resort.

Much later in 2004, we encountered monkeys near Ulu Waatu in Bali. Tim and I were vacationing there with our youngest son, Scott, who had flown out from the States to meet us. We visited a temple area from where we could see the famed Ulu Waatu Temple, which perched on a rocky promontory and jutted out into the sea.

A sign greeted us at the entrance to the long climb up to the temple. The sign warned us about the resident monkeys and told us to remove anything from our person that could be removed: hats, sunglasses, eyeglasses, keys, earrings, necklaces, bracelets, etc. Being the obedient soul that I am, I removed my glasses, watch, and jewelry and prepared to climb to the top. Tim and Scott read the same warning but chose to keep their glasses on because they claimed they couldn't see without them.

The climb to the top of the hill was breathtaking as the setting sun burnished the bougainvillea and provided a stark contrast to the black rocks and blue water down below the vertiginous cliff. It was the perfect picture opportunity.

On the climb up, I had been wary of the monkeys that huddled in groups along the path or scampered among the stones of the temple. When Scott lined Tim and me up for a picture beside the stone wall overlooking the sheer drop to the sea below, I was aware there was a monkey sitting on that same wall approximately six feet away from us.

Scott kept trying to focus and get the perfect shot (a near-impossible task with his parents as subjects) while taking his sweet time doing it. As Scott fiddled with the camera, the monkey edged closer.

"Hurry up, Scott," I said. The next thing I remember was a blur of brown and the sound of my screams as the monkey lunged for Tim's glasses and disappeared over the side of the cliff. It all happened in a matter of seconds.

Those had been relatively new glasses and expensive ones, at that. Somehow, I seemed to be more indignant than Tim was at the loss of his glasses. Nearby tourists and locals who were visiting the temple seemed to be enjoying our dilemma as long as it wasn't happening to them. Finally, an Indonesian man came to our rescue by offering to go over the side of the cliff to retrieve Tim's glasses. From my point of view, going over the cliff and risking a fall onto the rocks 500 feet below didn't seem worth the retrieval of the glasses. Nevertheless, he persisted and disappeared over the cliff after the monkey.

After what seemed like an interminable length of time, he reappeared over the rock wall, holding Tim's glasses with a triumphant look on his face. We were thrilled to get the glasses back, thanked him profusely, and rewarded him handsomely. Tim promptly put his glasses back on.

Only later did we come to understand that the Indonesian man and the monkey were in cahoots. The monkey had been trained to snatch items off unsuspecting tourists (glasses were a favorite), and that's the way the man made his living. The monkey's payment was a few bananas. What could be more ingenious than that?

Based on these first-hand experiences, I now steer clear of monkeys whenever I can. I cannot be tempted to visit Monkey Forest when we're in Ubud, Bali. Nor do we plan on taking a tour of Monkey Island when we visit Phuket, Thailand later this month. No, sir, no amount of convincing will get me to change my opinion of those nasty creatures. How did I ever think otherwise?

§

After the first year in Indonesia, Tim and I planned to return to the U.S. for R & R. I went ahead, and Tim planned to follow after a few weeks. We would spend some time with our boys in the Washington, D.C. area and then fly to Portland, Oregon to reconnect with extended family in Oregon and Washington.

Two days after I arrived home from Jakarta, I found myself at the vet's office with our cat, Kaydu. Scott had e-mailed me back in February that Kaydu had a sore on her tummy, and she wouldn't let him touch her there. I e-mailed back that he should take her into the vet, and I gave him the name and address of our vet in Vienna. That didn't happen, so when I came home, taking Kaydu to the vet was the first item on my agenda.

Kaydu was my cat. She had always been my cat because she recognized that I was the one who had rescued her from a life of deprivation on the streets of Cairo. I found myself in the vet's examining room facing a female vet I had never seen before, who became increasingly concerned as she palpated Kaydu's tummy. She announced that Kaydu had multiple mammary tumors and at Kaydu's advanced age of 15, the kindest thing to do would be to put her asleep. I was devastated upon hearing this news.

The vet said she could perform the procedure and it would be a painless death. I stood there next to the stainless steel examining table with tears in my eyes as I stroked Kaydu's face, ears, and body. I reassured my kitty that everything would be all right. I agreed with the vet that it would be cruel to put Kaydu through surgery at her age, especially knowing that Kaydu's body was now riddled with tumors in the advanced stage of cancer.

I agreed to the vet's plan, but when she asked if I wanted to call anyone to give me moral support for this unenviable task, my mind raced through the list of possible people I could call. Who could I call? Both Scott and Brian were working and probably couldn't get away for their cat's death. Was Susan, my friend from Cairo, at home? Maybe I could call Yeshi, who lived just down the street from the vet's office. She had a beloved Dachshund when we had both lived in the same apartment complex in Cairo.

In tears, I called everyone on my short list. It's at times like these that you most treasure friends you've made overseas. Yeshi said she'd come as soon as she could. Susan gave the same response. Scott said he'd try to get away, but Brian told me he couldn't. By the time Yeshi had arrived, out of breath because she had hurriedly walked down Nutley Street to where the vet's office was located, I was resigned to having to put Kaydu to sleep. There was such finality in the decision, and the tears continued to roll down my face. I hoped Kaydu knew I was trying to do what was best for her and that she wouldn't be in any more pain.

The lady vet was kind as she administered the medicine that caused Kaydu to pass away peacefully. The vet's experience had convinced her that pets do indeed have a soul and that there was a pet heaven. By this time, Susan and Scott had arrived as well as Harry, Yeshi's husband. They all consoled me through hugs and reassurances that I had done what was best for Kaydu.

After we left the vet's office we drove to Harry and Yeshi's house, just down the street, where we sat around their living room reminiscing about our time together in Cairo and the lives of our pets. Susan had three Siamese cats, and Yeshi and Harry had their dog, so it didn't seem too strange to sit there grieving Kaydu's passing. We had a cat wake.

The day after I had to put Kaydu to sleep, I found myself sitting in the orthopedic surgeon's office watching him as he manipulated my ankle. I had made an appointment with the surgeon to have him look at my left ankle, which still troubled me two years after having had surgery to insert pins in my ankle to hold the tibia together. I had experienced a vertical stress fracture in my left ankle bone. A small tear in my post-tibial tendon had also been repaired. Perhaps I only needed to get new inserts in my shoes to make walking easier.

I couldn't believe my ears when the doctor told me that my tendon was detached. How does one detach a tendon without feeling it? I would need more surgery, this time a tendon transfer from my little toes to my ankle to give me a functioning tendon. When I asked him to look at my right knee which I was unable to straighten, he sent me to have it x-rayed. It's never a good omen when a surgeon exhales air in a "whew" sound when looking at your x-ray films displayed on the light board in front of him.

I was dumbfounded when he said he couldn't repair the tendon of my left ankle until he gave me a total knee replacement of my right knee. I needed at least one good leg to stand on. Apparently, I had worn through the cartilage of my right knee by favoring my left ankle. I had no cartilage left, and the two bones of my right leg were rubbing together, which produced the pain I had been feeling. I needed to schedule the knee-replacement surgery right away; the second ankle surgery could be scheduled four months after the knee replacement.

I was literally shell shocked by this news, and it meant that all our summer plans flew out the window right then and there. I couldn't return to work in Jakarta. Tim would have to accelerate his plan to join me in Virginia. As Tim was the only American direct-hire in Aceh, he could only be absent for two weeks for the surgery itself and the difficult period following surgery.

I remember getting in the car to drive home after hearing the news, but I don't really remember seeing the red light on the main street leading from the hospital. It wasn't until I was halfway through the intersection and had seen the transit bus in the peripheral vision of my left eye that I realized what I had done. I quickly slammed on the brakes, looked in my rearview mirror, and backed up out of the intersection to allow the bus to proceed. Fortunately, there was no one behind me. My heart was beating erratically from what could have been, and I realized I was not thinking straight. The news of my two surgeries, having had to put Kaydu to sleep the day before, and my jet lag, had all permeated my consciousness, and I realized I had been simply operating on autopilot. I thanked God I had not been hit by the bus, necessitating a third surgery.

I had much need of the Celtic prayer, "If God sends you down a stony path, may he give you strong shoes."[11] Those strong shoes were a pair of brown, lace-up men's Keens, which I had worn since before my first ankle surgery in October 2007. I had discovered in searching for sturdy shoes that manufacturers didn't make women's shoes wide enough to accommodate the several different types of ankle braces I had to wear. I had to resort to buying men's shoes, although the Keens I bought at REI looked very much like women's walking shoes, only wider.

I had knee-replacement surgery in August 2009. After three days in the hospital, I came home to our townhouse and took up residence in the basement in Scott's bedroom. Scott was relegated to our upstairs bedroom to sleep on the floor. We had packed out most of our belongings before going to Indonesia, and the only furniture that remained in the house was one recliner in the living room, a TV and recliner in the basement, and Scott's bedroom furniture. Scott had a bathroom located right next door to his bedroom, and we thought that the basement level would be the most convenient one for me.

There was a friend at church, Judith, who had also had a knee replacement the year before, and she said that if I could make it through the first two weeks, everything would be all right. I lived each day hoping to make it through to that two-week mark. In addition to the pain and sleeplessness, I had to endure for 21 days the twice daily shots in the stomach of Lovenox, a blood thinner that helped prevent blood clots. Lovenox was a misnomer if I had ever heard one, for there was nothing even remotely related to love in those shots. For the first two weeks, Tim administered the shots, and for the next week, Scott gave them to me. I was glad that Scott had his EMT training, and I knew he would be good at it. A good shot was one that I barely felt, but even with an abundance of "good shots," by the end of the three-week period, my stomach was one massive bruise of black and blue as well as purple fading to yellow – a virtual Jackson Pollock of color.

I had put Tim through his paces, getting him up with me every few hours and either helping me to the bathroom or giving me my medicine. At the end of those two weeks with very little sleep himself, I'm sure he was eager to go back to Indonesia, where he could get a good night's sleep. I felt that if we could survive those two weeks with our marriage intact, we could survive anything.

---

[11] From John Birch, www.faithandworship.com

The breakthrough came with Judith's visit. She came on a Friday afternoon, equipped with a bottle of blowing bubbles and her knowledge of the musculature of the human body. As a former physical education teacher, she looked at me and could tell that I was hunching my shoulders from the pain, which was where my pain resided. That afternoon was heavenly as she gave me a back rub, walked me around the living room, and then took me out to the back deck, where we could sit in the sunshine and blow bubbles. She knew, although I didn't at the time, that the act of blowing bubbles would recalibrate my breathing and get me to stop holding my breath from the pain. Blowing bubbles seemed like such a silly thing to do that I couldn't help but laugh at myself and the situation. It felt so good to laugh. She later read me to sleep as I lounged in our overstuffed chair, which I had christened, my "throne."

Although I had been doing the knee exercises and bending my knee at home, I still wore an extensive knee brace to prevent my knee from rolling inward. After five weeks I began physical therapy once again to regain the strength and flexibility in my right knee.

In early December 2009 I returned to Jakarta to join Tim and to finish teaching my classes. By this time, Tim had decided that he wanted to make Indonesia a two-year post. This is what I wrote shortly after hearing about that decision.

A Look Back

It was 3 a.m. on an early Saturday morning in Jakarta, Indonesia as I sat there typing this sentence. I had just endured a week of amoebiasis histolytica, or amoebic dysentery by its more common, garden-variety name. I had the flat-on-the-floor, puking-in-a-bowl experience, and it was hard to gain some perspective on this occupational hazard of Foreign Service life. Six days into it, my stomach still felt like a toxic dump, and the miasma revisited me as heartburn. On the plus side, I had lost seven pounds. Intestinal illnesses were common in the Foreign Service, and I could count these stomach bugs among the more interesting flora and fauna that had at one time or the other, taken up residence in my gut: salmonella, shigella, cryptospora, giardiasis, amoebic dysentery (twice), and campylobacter. I rattled them off, reliving the experiences, and trotted them out like battle scars whenever expatriate talk turned to the tummy rumbles. They were almost like trading cards...Well, when I was in Pakistan...

My husband's plane in Banda Aceh, which is located on the northern tip of the island of Sumatra, 1,000 miles away from Jakarta, had been delayed due to engine trouble. He might not get home this weekend for his once-a-month visit to Jakarta because the airline couldn't find another plane, and all the flights out of Aceh were fully booked. It might have had something to do with the weather – this was the height of the monsoon season, and floodwaters were expected to peak this weekend. I was working and living in Jakarta, while he was working and living in Aceh because the U.S. Government, in its wisdom, had decided not to allow dependents in Aceh due to its occasionally dicey status as a post-conflict area.

I picked up an old friend, Richard, at the Jakarta airport that day and introduced him to the living situation in Jakarta and peripherally, to the work situation at USAID, where he would work a three-month contract setting up an environmental strategy and program for USAID/Indonesia.

We had known Richard and his wife, Patty, since 1990, when we were living in our first post, Islamabad, Pakistan. Our two families were on a trip to the Khyber Pass, that historic gateway separating Afghanistan and Pakistan, when we discovered Richard and I shared a birthday – November 23. Since that time, we had celebrated many birthdays together and had fond memories of birthday dinners at a fancy French restaurant overlooking the Nile in Cairo or at a French country inn in McLean, Virginia. French food seemed to be the common denominator. Coincidentally, another close friend and USAID spouse, Naida, shared the same birthday. Now, whenever we were in the same time zone, the three couples celebrated together.

I told Richard I was sorry to say he wasn't joining one big, happy family at USAID/Indonesia. Although I was on the periphery by virtue of being the writing instructor for the USAID foreign nationals there and not privy to information within the inner circle, it seemed that all the direct hires and contractors just put their heads down and worked. Our ranks at USAID worldwide had been decimated over the years due to budget cuts, hiring freezes, and political disfavor, and now we were operating at half-staff but doing more work. Seasoned officers had been cherry-picked to fill critical-priority positions in Afghanistan, Pakistan, Iraq, and Sudan. Those who were left at post were working flat-out to take up the slack.

Tim had been mulling our situation over and had decided that we would most likely make Indonesia a two-year post rather than a four-year one. By July 2010, we will have been separated for three years, and it was too much of a personal sacrifice in our marriage. This was our second unaccompanied tour; our first was Afghanistan. Couples tended to grow apart and, out of necessity, developed their own lives. We were missing important family time that could never be replaced. Tim didn't want to return to the pressure cooker of USAID/Washington, nor did he want to go to another unaccompanied hardship post such as Sudan, where his food aid skills would most be needed.

Although I'd always thought of our life overseas as an enchanted one, perhaps that was a misnomer; maybe what I'd been experiencing lately was disenchantment rather than enchantment.

On second thought, maybe I shouldn't have left this on such a sour note. Despite my momentary attitude of sour grapes, I realized that I had attained a milestone of sorts. A month earlier we had been sitting at the Jakarta airport at Starbucks (across from Krispy Kreme) waiting for our flight to Singapore. Our plans were to spend the Christmas holiday in Singapore and to experience more of the Christmas spirit than was evident in Jakarta. As I was sipping my tea, I became aware that I no longer felt strange sitting there. I noticed that the people around me looked normal and that I was a part of a normal landscape, too. The buzz of conversation around me was distinguishable, and I could understand a good part of it. I looked at all the black hair and Asian features on the people around us, and I felt like Tim and I were two errant sesame seeds on a poppy seed bun. This was good.

Indonesia at first glance would seem to be the ideal posting. It was a moderate Islamic country that had managed to survive the current worldwide economic downturn with a minimum of chaos. Its currency, the rupiah, had not in the recent past experienced the widespread fluctuations that had devastated the country in 1998. It had a relatively stable government that had been democratically elected. Minorities had experienced increased freedoms in the past few years – freedoms unheard of ten or more years ago. The Indonesians of ethnic Chinese origin could now worship freely and could celebrate Chinese New Year as well as study the Chinese dialects and history of their forefathers. Public dissent was now more acceptable and tolerated.

Indonesia had also made great strides in promoting national unity among its ethnic groups living in this archipelago of more than 17,000 islands spanning over 3,000 miles. Indonesia now experienced journalistic freedom and had an open press that reported without too much censure in its many newspapers and television stations. I contrasted the lack of censure in Indonesia to the time we were living in Malaysia as Peace Corps Volunteers in the late 1970s. Our *Time* magazines would arrive with thick black markings covering the pages, which blotted out whatever the censors had objected to. Photos of scantily clad women were considered especially objectionable.

Indonesia had had moderate success in tamping down the spread of terrorism, and its cities and towns were for the most part, safe for its citizens. Although the tug-and-pull of fundamentalism versus moderation still existed among the Muslim communities, there was, in most places, an acceptance of "otherness" that allowed the individual to dress, worship, and behave as he or she saw fit. Indonesia was a relatively easy country for an expat to live in.

What surprised me most about Jakarta was learning that life was lived in the air-conditioned malls. Jakarta was a congested metropolis of approximately 13 million people with few parks and recreational outdoor opportunities. Fancy malls had sprung up and contained all the amenities modern residents needed or wanted: restaurants from around the world; movie theaters where you could recline with a pillow and blanket while watching your favorite flick; arcades geared to pre-teens and teens; upscale shops like Gucci and Yves St. Laurent; pricey grocery stores that carried imported items; bookstores that stocked bestsellers in English and Bahasa; and children's play areas, complete with carousels and child-sized working trains.

Everyone made a pilgrimage to the malls on the weekends to window shop, eat out, and enjoy the day. One of the malls, Grand Indonesia, had floors that resembled theme parks, where you could shop in a retro New York atmosphere complete with street signs, fake subway cars, and billboards advertising the laundry detergent, Cheer, and Clark bars – all with the song, "New York, New York" blasting over the loudspeakers. To complete the kitsch, the restrooms, which were modeled on subway trains and had sleek stainless steel interiors, sported a picture of Marlon Brando or Marilyn Monroe on the doors. In Jakarta, rarely did people get outdoors to receive even the recommended minimum of 15 minutes of sunshine per day to produce the vitamin D needed for their bodies. The younger generation in the cities has been raised in malls, and it remains to be seen how this will affect Indonesian society on a wide scale.

American and other foreign eateries abounded, and you could go from Hard Rock Café to California Pizza Kitchen to Dairy Queen and more. That is if you could afford it. The prices in the restaurants rivaled prices back home, so only the wealthy could eat out at the foreign eateries. Most expats packed on the pounds in Indonesia and found it hard to maintain their weight, despite the occasional intestinal parasite.

Although there were malls galore there in Jakarta, I longed for the ability to walk into a store and find clothing that fit. I felt like one of the Brobdingnagians of <u>Gulliver's Travels</u> compared to the Indonesians' Lilliputians. Indonesian designers had not caught on to the fact that western women were larger than Indonesian women; in fact, I had found only two stores in all of Jakarta that carried larger sizes. The "large" women's size in Indonesian stores corresponded to a size 10 in American sizes. I felt like a cow going into an Indonesian store and being told by the size-two sales clerk that they didn't carry anything in my size. I'd had too many opportunities to practice the superlative in Bahasa Indonesia in asking for "yang paling besar" – the largest size – only to be confronted with a mumu-type garment that looked like something that Omar the Tentmaker crafted. On occasion when I found something that fit, I had to buy a 4X. In the U.S. at size 14, I was normal; in Indonesia, I was gargantuan.

The more well-to-do families employed one or more nannies to mind the children, so it was common to see young Indonesian women in white uniforms carrying infants in batik slings or pushing strollers and tagging along behind the parents while on a shopping expedition. Sometimes there was one nanny (ayah) per child, and you would often see parents trailed by their entourage of nannies and children.

While it was true that life in the big cities was lived in the malls, Indonesia also boasted of being an island paradise. Bali to me was a little piece of heaven if you could get away from the more touristy areas where the young crowd congregated. Scratch a Balinese and you would find an artist; in fact, the majority of people in Bali were descended from the artist class of Hindus, who fled the Islamic incursion into Indonesia centuries earlier.

When driving throughout Bali, one could see the evidence of this artistic heritage every 500 meters: silversmiths, wood carvers, egg painters, stone masons, batik weavers, and oil painters. Bali was also a feast for the eyes in its natural beauty with its Hindu temples with fruit-carrying worshipers and lush greenery along the roadside.

Despite these pluses to living in Indonesia, my husband and I found ourselves longing for a return to our roots and life as we knew it before joining the Foreign Service. I longed for a return to four seasons and a respite from always being hot and sweaty. I longed to wear a sweater. I missed being able to blend in to the background and to go incognito when I was out in public. We missed being around our boys and being a part of their lives. We couldn't tell you how many weddings and births we had missed in our families. I missed being able to turn over in bed and feel the warm embrace of Tim's arms as we slept spoon-fashion. Perhaps all of these longings were part of the natural transition we needed to make in the mental shift from what was to what could be.

When Tim first broached the subject of retirement, I was resistant and fearful. After all, it was difficult to contemplate life after 22 years in USAID. How would you give up a known for an unknown? I had become a product of the USAID culture as much as Tim, for my life had been equally circumscribed by his employment with USAID. What would life look like after USAID? How could he give up his life's work while still in his productive years? Given the current worldwide economic crisis, would we have enough money to live on in retirement? How would we deal with a return to anonymity after living a visible, somewhat pampered life? Would we still be able to travel? Because I was much more employable overseas than in the States, would I be able to find a job where I was valued for my skills and abilities? Would he be content not working?

While contemplating these questions and fears, I sat and pondered the what-ifs and the what-nows. Tim was several steps ahead of me in the process for the reason that he was currently disenchanted with his work, which was in a closeout phase, and his life in Aceh. In retirement, he would be improving his circumstances, which had severely restricted him in Aceh. For him, his next posting would most likely be Washington again, which he was not looking forward to. He had also witnessed several of his colleagues keel over with a heart attack or stroke shortly after retirement, and he didn't want that to happen to him. Neither did I.

For me, life was not so bad, despite the separation, and I'd come to enjoy my job as writing instructor and the life I lived there in Jakarta. I had access to many more amenities, and I was not as restricted socially as Tim was. I had friends there in our apartment complex, and life was relatively easy.

Over the previous several months while contemplating retirement, I'd discovered that this transition was merely a more expanded version of the transition that you made when transferring to a new post. In the move to a new post, you started to read and invest yourself mentally in it and in all practicality, disengaged from your current life and post six months prior to moving.

In one book I'd read, <u>Practical Dreamers</u>, an analogy was made between the mental process required in reading a novel and that of contemplating the unknown future. As you turned the pages of a novel, gradually you began to invest yourself in the characters' lives until at some point you became totally immersed in the book, living vicariously along with the characters. Contemplating the unknown future was similar in that you gradually divested yourself of the present until the future seemed more possible. I could do this.

If we retired we could see the boys more often, not just during the summer months while we were on home leave. We would be closer to Tim's parents in Oregon, who were going through their own transition in moving from their home of 52 years to a retirement home. We would be closer to my only sister, who lived in Olympia, Washington. We would be closer to extended family in the Pacific Northwest and could get together more frequently. Tim would be relieved from the pressures of work, particularly those that involved personnel issues. He had discovered that as he progressed through the ranks of USAID, the higher he went, the more paperwork, and human resource, administrative, and policy decisions he had to make. He'd always been a field man, and as he became more distanced from seeing the results of his work in the field, the more disenchanted he became.

Tim gave notice that he wanted to retire and leave Aceh, and he was fortunate this decision coincided with the closeout of USAID's Aceh office. Tim had originally been sent to Aceh to oversee the closing of USAID's programs there because it had been five years since the tsunami, and Aceh had in many ways, come back stronger than it had been before the disaster.

The capital city of Banda Aceh had been rebuilt and there was a formal peace agreement in place signed by the government in Jakarta and the rebels, who wanted greater autonomy for Aceh. The conflict had been simmering for 30 years, but when the province of Aceh lost more than 125,000 of its inhabitants and parts of Banda Aceh were wiped off the map due to the destruction by the tsunami, the opposing parties saw the event as an act of God. Maybe God was telling them to put away their animosities and work together for the betterment of their province. Surely they needed everyone in the province to apply themselves to the monumental task needed to recover from the devastation. There was no more time for fighting; they needed to pull together and rebuild their lives.

The timing of the decision to retire was ultimately good for me as well. My students were progressing well in their writing skills. Some of them had even written articles about development issues that had been published on the USAID/Indonesia Web site. I was proud of their achievements and felt that they had come a long way in their course of study. Maybe it was time for me to leave also.

Although it's difficult leaving post and the friends you've made there, there's a realization that you might see those friends again, for you discover that your USAID friends keep going around and around in the system, moving from one post to another. Eventually, they'll all wind up at some point at the Mother Ship in Washington, D.C., where you can see them again, even if you're now retired. We were going home; it's always easier to be the one leaving post than the one who's left behind because we were embarking on a new adventure, and we had our family to go home to.

Although I had recovered from the knee replacement surgery, my left ankle still pained me after walking for more than two hours, despite my taking physical therapy in Jakarta. My physician back home convinced me that I should go to a foot and ankle specialist who might be able to solve my tendon problem. I made an appointment to see an orthopedic surgeon who specialized in feet and ankles and even lectured at Georgetown University on the subject.

Chapter Seven • Washington State

O God, help me to follow you wherever you may lead me... I was relieved after seeing the specialist to hear him say that he wanted to find out why my tendon had torn. After doing tests and looking at the results, he came to the conclusion that my tendon had torn because my foot and ankle were out of alignment. What he needed to do was to restructure both my foot and ankle so the tendon transfer he performed would not result in the tendon tearing again. I was relieved to know that someone was paying closer attention to my problem this time around.

Surgery was scheduled for June 9 at 10:30 a.m. This date and time for my surgery turned out to be one of those "thin places," where I was to experience the certainty of God's presence. I had not been very enthusiastic about undergoing yet another surgery to repair the damage from the first ankle surgery, but I came to understand that the timing had been divinely appointed because of the synchronicity of it all.

I discovered in corresponding with my good friend, Elcye, that she, too, would have surgery on June 9 at 10:30 a.m. Elcye had recently been told she had breast cancer, and she would have a mastectomy in South Carolina at that time and on that date. We both marveled at the timing of it all, and we surmised that Elcye's brother, Bill, who had passed away a year earlier, was up in heaven orchestrating the events. Bill was an Episcopal priest, who had come out to visit us twice in Cairo, and we were very fond of him. For Elcye and me, it was a relief to be able to take our minds off our own worries and instead, pray for the other. I thought having a mastectomy was much more serious than my foot and ankle surgery. Elcye thought just the opposite. Knowing that a good friend was undergoing surgery at the same time allowed both of us to feel less anxious about our own situation. We both chuckled at the image of Father Bill up in heaven watching over us and directing his fellow angels to work on our behalf.

My surgery was an out-patient surgery that lasted 2 ½ hours. When I first met the doctor post-surgery, he told me all he had done in that short period of time. He had removed the bunion and straightened the big toe; done a tendon transfer from the little toes to the ankle; broken the arch of my foot to give me a more pronounced arch; cut my heel in half in order to move my heel over, and lengthened my Achilles' heel tendon. I now had seven pieces of metal in my left foot and ankle. He said there had been more work for him to do than he had anticipated, but still, I thought it was remarkable to have done what he did in that short period of time.

I had to be non-weight bearing for seven weeks following surgery, and I returned to the basement bedroom of our townhouse in Virginia once again. After hopping around on one foot and using a walker, I was finally able to put weight on my foot and began another round of physical therapy to regain greater function and flexibility. By the end of seven weeks of dusting the steps with my butt up to the main floor and the kitchen, I was ready for more freedom and a return to normalcy! One benefit to being non-weight bearing, however, was that my arms and shoulders became quite strong in supporting my body weight on one foot while pushing the walker in front of me.

My goal was to be able to attend my nephew, Michael's, wedding in Twin Falls, Idaho in August. I encouraged our oldest son, Brian, to accompany me to the wedding to help me out and to represent the Mattson side of the family. I knew our family would be sparsely represented.

Michael and Brooke's wedding was a glorious affair and was held in her uncle's back yard. My sister, Lindy, was so glad to have both Brian and me at the wedding. She mentioned over and over that she was delighted that she could attend Michael's wedding and that he would have a new family. Michael was marrying into a Mormon family, whose family ties were strong. They had readily accepted Michael into their clan and welcomed him as one of their own.

My sister, Lindy, had suffered from rheumatoid arthritis for over 40 years and had been through so many surgeries she was a bionic woman – artificial knees and hips, fingers and toes. The arthritis had disfigured her joints and had made doing even simple daily tasks like dressing, painful. While on the trip to Salt Lake, she had fallen in the bathroom of the hotel and had further injured her joints. She was in a lot of pain, but she radiated a glow reflecting the pride she felt in seeing Michael married. She was so happy. Little did I know at the time that Lindy's comments about her living to see Michael married were prescient in that they represented her final, big achievement in life.

We were quite the pair, and I wondered what Brooke's family thought about the family she was marrying into. My sister walked to the front row of seats on crutches; I was in a boot from my surgery and was using a cane. Michael and Brian were the only Mattson family members in good health. Lindy's husband, Leon, had to forego attending the wedding because he had had an inner ear disturbance and had to lay flat on his back to recover from it.

After the wedding, Brian and I flew back to Virginia, and Tim and I prepared to put the house up for sale in preparation for our move to Washington State. Tim had attended the Retirement Seminar for Foreign Service Officers in D.C., where he had learned about the emotional, physical, and financial impact of retirement decisions. One of the lessons they stressed in the seminar was to choose a retirement location based on your needs, not one that took into account your children's locations. They stated that our children were more mobile than we were, and we shouldn't choose a place to retire based on where our children lived. They would move to follow a job.

Our boys at that time were still in the Washington, D.C. area. Brian was attending school at St. John's College in Annapolis, Maryland, and Scott was working in the Crystal City area in Virginia.

There were many criteria to consider as we debated where to retire. We knew that we couldn't continue to live in Oakton and not work. The high cost of living and our mortgage payment would make it impossible to retire without both of us continuing to work in professional positions. We wanted a smaller community with less traffic. We wanted a college town with a smaller population. Proximity to an airport was also important in case Tim were to take short-term contracts and continue his line of work. We wanted to be within easy driving distance of extended family. Tim's parents as well as his older brother and younger sister and their families all lived in the Portland, Oregon area.

My number one priority was being near my sister; she and I were the sole survivors of our nuclear Mattson family. We both wanted a small city with a much lower cost of living. Tim had crunched the numbers and based on our projected retirement income of 40% of our pre-retirement income, we needed to find a community that was much less expensive to live in. Based on these factors, we chose the Olympia, Washington area. Both my sister and I were happy we would again live in close proximity to each other.

Tim and I were surprised when our townhouse sold within a month, despite the slow real estate market in general. We learned that the old adage, location, location, location was true, and we were thankful our townhouse was located at the end of the Orange Line, which made it attractive to would-be buyers. We had just a short two-week window to find another house to live in while the sale was concluded and the paperwork on the house closed. By this time, we had located a realtor in Olympia, who agreed to meet us as soon as we arrived in town and show us housing that met our criteria. Tim and I, independently of each other, had created a list of the priorities we wanted in a house.

We wanted a one-level house that was not very old. Neither of us was any good at home repairs. We thought at one point my sister might come to live with us, so we also needed wide hallways, wide enough to accommodate a wheelchair. There couldn't be more than one or two steps to the front door. We needed at least three bedrooms and two bathrooms. We wanted to be in a neighborhood with sidewalks and lights and close to public transportation. We both wanted a fireplace and a garage. We didn't want a very large yard because of the upkeep required, although I wanted a small space for a garden, where I could grow flowers. A front porch would be ideal, and I wanted windows that opened and closed easily. Being in a safe neighborhood was also a top priority. Hardwood floors were also on our wish list so we could display our oriental rugs. Was this too much to ask?

We took off from Virginia in our red Honda on our week-long driving trip across the States. The plan was to leave one vehicle in Portland with Tim's parents and then return to Virginia by Amtrak to complete the closing on our townhouse and pack out. I had never driven cross-country before, and I looked forward to the trip. We had beautiful weather throughout the six-day trip, and we managed to cover 500 miles a day. We realized that although we had seen much of the world in our Foreign Service life, we had not been tourists in our own country. Driving from state to state showed us the beauty and diversity of our country, and we drove past place names that up to that point had only been dots on the map: Cumberland Gap, Akron, Chicago, Bismarck, Cheyenne, and Wallace, Idaho, to name just a few.

We were most impressed by the State of South Dakota. When we reached the eastern border of the state, we stopped at one of their tourist centers, where we bought a four-part CD we played in our car's CD player. The CDs recounted the history and geography of the area as we reached each milepost of the road. We learned that Tom Brokaw was a South Dakota son, while Laura Ingalls Wilder had at one point lived in a sod house on the prairie in that state. The South Dakota tourism bureau definitely had its act together. If you bought the set of CDs for $20, you could mail them back once you reached your destination and receive a $15 refund. Our investment of $5 proved to be most enlightening and entertaining on the long drive across the state, and we wished other states had done the same in promoting the history and geography of their area.

Finally we reached Olympia. Our realtor, Connie, was well prepared, and we viewed approximately two dozen homes in our three-day stay. Our time in the Olympia area was curtailed because we needed to be in Portland to board Amtrak for our return home. We finally found a house in the Stikes Woods area of Lacey, which met all our criteria. The current owner was a do-it-yourself kind of guy, and he had recently renovated the kitchen with granite countertops, tile flooring, and beautiful cabinetry. He had made other major improvements such as wood flooring, built-in cabinets in the living room, and tile flooring in the bathrooms and the hallway. He had even installed surround sound in the living room for a large-screen TV. He had a gas fireplace installed as well with beautiful slate surrounding the fireplace. To top it off, the colors he had painted the house were not garish but ones we really liked in taupe and yellow. The house was move-in ready, and it seemed like it was meant just for us. We put an offer on the house and made the sale contingent on a house inspection, which our realtor would attend in our place. We had a train to catch in Portland.

We were dismayed to receive the inspection report from our realtor via e-mail when our train was delayed in Chicago. The report totaled 36 pages of irregularities and exceptions. Although the current owner did beautiful work, he had neglected to obtain the necessary permits from the city's inspectors for his improvements. Sadly, we had to withdraw our bid because we couldn't see buying the house and later having to get the necessary permits ourselves after-the-fact if we ever needed to sell the house.

At that point, the seller decided to get into gear, and he said he would retroactively obtain the necessary permits required by the city. Our realtor later told us that the city inspector had never seen anyone more proactive and motivated in doing the work required to obtain all the necessary building permits within two weeks. Finally, we received word that he had gotten all the permits, and we resubmitted our bid, which was accepted. We eagerly looked forward to moving into our new home.

We arrived in Lacey two weeks before the house closed, and we took possession on December 1, 2010. Our household shipments were scheduled for December 2, December 3, and December 10. The first two shipments were from Jakarta and from Virginia, where we had left minimal furniture during our time overseas. The majority of our household effects came out of storage in Virginia. This shipment we received on December 10.

The challenge was to try and put away each shipment in order to be able to receive the bulk of our shipment on December 10. We also wanted to put the house in order before our boys arrived on December 21 to spend Christmas with us. It would be the first Christmas we had spent together as a family for perhaps ten years, and we wanted it to be a good one. Tim and I worked like fiends to be able to get the house ready for the boys. We were even able to put some Christmas decorations up before the boys arrived. We hoped our sons would become attached to our new home and that they would consider it their home, too.

I remember one evening when I had become exhausted from opening box after box and being faced with mountains of belongings we had no space for. I decided to focus instead on our Nepali dollhouse, which was a more manageable task. I un-wrapped the furniture for our three-story dollhouse and put together each room – bedroom, living room, dining room, attic, and even bathroom. The outside of the house was decorated as well with a Chinese gong on the steps leading to the front door, which was framed by a Nepali wood carving; there was even a chicken coop with chickens and geese next to the well and the snow-covered wall made of stones. These outside decorations were placed under the three tall white-flocked trees that represented The Himalayas. I strung a set of lights around the miniature Christmas tree in the living room of the dollhouse and put the wooden Nepali people in place. There. They were all moved in. It was ironic that our Nepali people had their house put together before Tim and I did.

We eagerly waited for the boys' arrival. Unfortunately, both boys arrived in Washington State with bad colds they had picked up on the flight out from Virginia. They were good sports, however, and we all drove down to Portland to celebrate Christmas with Tim's side of the family. It had been many years since both boys had seen their grandparents and their cousins. Unfortunately, we didn't visit my sister because she had a compromised immune system because of her illness. We didn't want her to catch the boys' colds, which could mean many months on antibiotics for her.

We had a lovely Christmas celebration with Brian and Scott, and as Tim and I drove home from Sea-Tac Airport after dropping the boys off, we looked forward to settling in to our new home and our new neighborhood.

In early January 2011 the weather was quite cold. On the night of January 3 I had difficulty sleeping, so I went out to the living room to sleep on the couch, where I wouldn't keep Tim awake. I had difficulties sleeping on the couch, too, so I spent a few hours of the early morning reading. In looking back, perhaps this was my third encounter with "thin places."

I never expected to receive a phone call from my brother-in-law, Leon, that morning of January 4 at 5:30 a.m. He kept repeating in an anguished voice, "She's dead. Lindy's dead." I had difficulty comprehending what had happened. How had she died? Why had she died? So much spilled out of Leon's mouth that I couldn't take it all in, but I felt we needed to go over to their house as quickly as possible. I, too, had difficulty relating the terrible news to Tim between my sobs, but as we hurriedly dressed, I knew we needed to be with Leon to console him.

In my grief and shock, I had forgotten to ask Leon where my sister's body was. We tried calling his phone repeatedly, but there was no answer. I assumed that the ambulance had taken her to the hospital. We quickly drove through the cold, darkened streets to Providence St. Peter's Hospital and walked into the Emergency Room, which was deserted at that hushed hour except for one other person. After repeated inquiries, we discovered that no, they had not admitted anyone by my sister's name. It was a new experience for me to tell the receptionist that my sister had recently died, *died!* and I didn't know if anyone had taken her body to the hospital or not.

Tim and I drove over to Leon's house south of the airport. The door was unlocked, and Leon was sitting at the kitchen table in grief and tears trying to absorb the recent events. The EMTs were also there and together from Leon and the EMT staff, we learned about the events of that early morning when my sister had had difficulties breathing. She had taken a nebulizer treatment, but it had little or no effect, so she asked Leon to call an ambulance. By the time the ambulance arrived, Lindy was in respiratory failure, and she failed to respond to all measures to revive her. She lay on the bedroom floor where she had fallen.

That day turned out to be several days long as Leon, Tim, and I did what had to be done. Leon called Lindy's son, Michael, early that morning to tell him that his mother had passed away at the age of 62. Leon and I started planning Lindy's memorial service for January 11.

The service was held at St. Michael's church in Olympia. It was a lovely, small service with just a few family and friends present. My cousins, Kenny, his wife, Laura, and Garry Mattson, whom I hadn't seen in a long time also came, and we were able to reconnect after all those years. Lindy's son, Michael, and his new wife, Brooke, came from Twin Falls. Leon's son, Chris, flew in from Anchorage for the service to support his dad. Tim's parents, his brother, Steve, and Tim's sister, Melinda, and her husband, John, also came to give us their condolences. One of Lindy's oldest friends, Shirley, also came from Oregon. Roger and Cathy, also old friends, arrived from the Seattle area.

I had no heart for writing yet another eulogy after the ones I had written for my father and mother. Now, I was the only remaining member of our nuclear family, and I didn't know what to say. Finally, I remembered my favorite picture of Lindy, one in which she's standing by a fence in New Zealand and petting a sheep. She seemed so content and happy standing there talking to and petting the curly-haired sheep that had poked its head over the fence. It reminded me of the Lord's Prayer and the first line of that prayer – *"The Lord is my Shepherd, I shall not be in want."* (Psalm 23:1 NIV)

It reminded me of the stuffed animal that Tim had bought me in Jogjakarta, Indonesia. We had taken the escalator up the floors in a department store, when we reached the toy section. There in one of the bins was the cutest, cuddliest sheep I had ever seen. She had curly white ringlets all over her body, and her nose and eyes were black. She looked at me with such trusting eyes. Tim decided to buy her right then and there to replace the pillow I cuddled with at night. I called her Domba, the Indonesian word for sheep. I had shown Domba to Lindy when we had visited her and her husband, and I decided to get Lindy her own Domba. To me, Domba represented peace and safety.

My message in the eulogy was that now Lindy was with her Shepherd, and she would no longer want for anything. She would be in no more pain, and she would be like a tenderly loved sheep, watched over and cared for by her Savior.

I walked through the memorial service and reception afterwards at our house on autopilot, and curiously, with dry eyes. I don't remember what I said or what I did, but maybe those things were unimportant. The important thing that day was that we had all gathered to celebrate Lindy's life among us. I would miss her greatly, and I would grieve the time that had been taken from us, time we didn't have together after all those years apart.

This wasn't how it was supposed to work out. We had moved to Washington State to be closer to my sister. We had left our boys behind on the East Coast. What now, Lord? Why did You bring us to Lacey? What is Your plan for us now? Why did You bring us here only to let Lindy die a month later?

§

The Danish philosopher and theologian, Søren Kierkegaard, said that "Life can only be understood backwards; but it must be lived forwards." We're now living our life in retirement forwards, and we're trying to make sense of it all by looking backwards.

It's been almost three years since we arrived in Lacey, and we're still trying to find our niche, our place in this new life. We're trying to make our former life in USAID relevant to the life that we're now living. We're trying to connect with people of like minds, those who share our common interests in people from other cultures and countries. We're trying to make new friends, but we realize from our previous experiences that it's often a slow process. We've discovered that although people overseas make friends readily and easily, the process here in the U.S. is not as easy. I recognize my pattern in all of this – I'm never truly happy until I have at least one good female friend, someone whom I can call on the spur of the moment and ask if she'd like a cup of coffee.

I'm grateful to USAID for the life we were privileged to live overseas. We were able to see the world because of Tim's job; our boys became world citizens who saw and learned things that could only have come from first-hand encounters, not from books. In looking back, Tim and I realized by making the decision to join USAID, we made decisions for ourselves and our boys that had a tremendous impact on their lives.

For better or for worse, parents make decisions for their children. In contemplating the last 25 years, we think our decisions were for the better, but only time will tell. We're still waiting to see which son will follow the statistical model for Foreign Service kids raised overseas. Foreign Service psychiatrists often state that 50% of children raised as Third Culture Kids will want to permanently stay in the U.S., put down roots, and never leave. The other 50% of kids will become vagabonds like their parents. Will our boys follow that statistical pattern? At this point, Scott seems to be the homebody because he married Katy, a dentist who practices with her dad in Maryland. Dentists don't move, so we think Scott and Katy have permanently settled in Maryland. Brian, although he's now lived in the Los Angeles area for almost three years, we're not so sure of.

When I look back at our life overseas, I think of the word, serendipity. The <u>Oxford American Dictionary of Current English</u> defines serendipity as "the faculty of making happy and unexpected discoveries by accident." The adjective serendipitous is as apt a description as any to describe the life my husband and I have had since he joined USAID in 1988. It's not only been serendipitous, but it's been quite a ride – one that I could never have imagined for myself growing up in a small town in Wisconsin. Who knew we had the faculty for serendipity and that we were to see the world and be so blessed?

It's not that I credit ourselves for that serendipity, for I realize our blessings have come not from our own doing but as a gift from God. We have been abundantly graced. The question now, as it has always been, is what now? Why have You placed us here? What are we to do with these experiences? How are we to bless others in the same way we have been blessed?

The bigger questions of life I leave up to God, for I know that my puny brain could never comprehend the bigger whys of this life we have led. I liken myself to Winnie the Pooh, "O bear of little brain." I wonder why we spent the entirety of Tim's career in the Islamic world. We tried to live out our Christian beliefs, but we doubt we had much of an impact on any of the people we encountered at work, in our neighborhood, or even in our home. At most, we did what little we could by being generous to our household help and treating them justly. We helped Jobeida, who was a single mother of one son in Bangladesh, save enough money from her salary to buy a small piece of land near the area she grew up. She would finally have some security of her own, security that few single, uneducated Bangladeshi women had.

Tim in his job can point to perhaps a greater impact on the lives his work touched. As a Food Security and Disaster Management Officer, he and his colleagues were able to step into people's lives at crucial moments of their greatest need: times of floods, times of food scarcity, and times of devastation due to a tsunami.

English teachers never encounter emergencies, for which I am grateful, for I'm not as cool-headed as Tim is. My successes could be measured in small, incremental improvements in the language proficiency of my students, in the confidence they felt with their new-found fluency in speech or writing. It could be measured by the articles my students wrote about development in Indonesia, which were published on the USAID Web site. This gave me great satisfaction, but how can this success be measured? My efforts seemed less tangible than Tim's, not easily measured with scales or calculators.

It wasn't as easy for me as it was for Tim to count my successes, however small. He could measure his successes in the metric tons of grain shipped to starving people in the Horn of Africa during the Ethiopian famine. He could measure his success by the number of cyclone shelters constructed to mitigate the effects of the massive cyclones that hit the coastline in the Bay of Bengal. He could count the number of small businesses that sprang up in Aceh, especially women-owned businesses, which allowed female heads of families to support their children.

The biggest question about our life overseas was why we had spent those years all in the Islamic world. Certainly, we never once led anyone to Christ during our time abroad. Proselytizing was strictly forbidden, and in every country we lived in, trying to convert a Muslim to Christianity was against the law; it could result in our having to leave the country. Our only recourse was to live our Christian beliefs as a witness to others. We hoped we always presented the love of Christ in our dealings with people, but we know there were times we didn't. I often felt like a cracked vessel, but I hoped that Christ's life would shine through those cracks.

§

How are we to make sense of the years we lived among Muslims in Pakistan, Egypt, Bangladesh, Afghanistan, and Indonesia? We knew that the Muslims we lived among and worked with felt as fervently about the Koran as we did about our Bible. We knew from our reading of the Bible that the Way to the Father was through Jesus Christ, His Son. We knew Muslims believed that Jesus was merely a prophet, leading up to the last prophet, Mohammed. We knew that just as we believed the Bible was the inspired word of God, Muslims believed that God had breathed inspiration into the Koran, and most Muslims believed it to be the inviolate Word of God.

Tim and I had visited Boudhanath, a holy site in Kathmandu, Nepal, where Buddhist devotees would circumambulate seven times around the massive white stupa, which was crowned with all-seeing kohl-lined eyes. From the very tip of the stupa prayer flags fluttered in the breeze. Tibetan Buddhists believed that the prayers written on these prayer flags fluttered to heaven when the breezes blew across them.

How was I to make sense of the religions we encountered? As a "bear of little brain," I had not had formal theological training, and I was ignorant of the writings of famous philosophers, many whose works permeated Western thought and formed its very foundation. I had never taken a class on Comparative Religions. What was God's plan when he set the world in motion? Why did so many people turn to other religions, and why had the Christian population been decimated in the Holy Land? Why did Jews and Muslims fight over that small piece of territory in Jerusalem called Temple Mount? Why was Jerusalem home to three of the world's religions?

I had been tested time and again on the Meyers-Briggs Personality Type Indicator, and every time I received the same classification – INFJ. As an INFJ, I was an introverted, intuitive individual who processed reality mostly on the feeling spectrum rather than the thinking spectrum. I liked things to be tidy in my mind, and I didn't like ambiguity. I wanted to see things in black and white, not gray. I wanted answers to my questions, and I sought connections between seemingly unrelated occurrences. God made me this way, so I didn't think he'd look askance at my question asking.

I suppose that God saw me and my questions the same way I saw our sons' why questions when they were three years old. They would look up at me with such trusting faces and say, "Mommy, why is the sky blue, and why do zebras have stripes? Both Brian and Scott repeated endless why questions as they worked to put their understanding of the world in order. I guess I'm no different than my sons in that respect. I know that God looks at my grappling with these enormous questions with a tender heart. He accepts my never-ending struggles with these questions and doesn't take offense at them, just as I didn't take offense at our sons' questions.

Recently I read the book, <u>The Closing of the Muslim Mind, How Intellectual Suicide Created the Modern Islamist Crisis</u> by Robert Reilly. I had picked this book out of Brian's personal book collection, which he had left with us for safekeeping. Brian had had to sell his cherished, private library of hundreds of books on two occasions, and for his most recent move to Los Angeles after he graduated from St. John's College, he had left approximately 30 of his favorite books behind with us. I didn't know at the time that the book would answer so many of the questions I had been struggling with after having lived in the Islamic world. I came to view the book also as a good way to stave off Alzheimer's because it stretched my mind as few other books had done in its comparison of the antecedents to both Islamic and Christian current-day beliefs.

As I read the book, two-thirds of which dealt with a discussion of the crisis that emerged from the 9th-11th centuries between two competing Islamic theologians who espoused very different theologies of Islam, I began to understand how the Islam of modern-day countries came into being. I understood the basis for the belief in the phrase, Insha'Allah, which was so prevalent in the societies where we had lived. It helped explain the Islamic belief that God's will determined a person's actions minute by minute. I began to understand why the Arab world, which at one time had been the epicenter of scientific and intellectual thought, now lagged behind most other parts of the world. I learned how in Christianity, man could ask questions of God because man had been made in the image of God. In Islam, God was all powerful and inscrutable, and his actions couldn't be questioned.

§

As I pondered the questions in my heart, I came to understand how in many ways, Tim and I had come full circle. I remember our talks when in 1987 we had dreamed of hosting a home for missionaries when they returned to the U.S. for home leave. We thought we could provide a home-away-from-home where missionaries could relax from their never-ending round of talks at churches in their efforts to raise funds to support their missionary work overseas. Tim and I knew first-hand of the weariness that came after sleeping in a succession of beds during home leave. One summer, we counted 26 different beds over a two-month period.

In a sense, our dream of supporting Christian mission work has been fulfilled by our hosting of the church's missionary prayer group. We meet once a month in our home and pray for the three missionary families our church supports. We have developed a personal relationship with them that allows them to share their personal prayer needs with us, and we have seen tangible results from those prayers in the lives of the missionaries we pray for.

I realized that the certainty I had felt in our early years of marriage concerning our settling down and not being able to achieve the American Dream was unfounded. We did settle down, and we have been blessed with our version of the American Dream. We have lived for almost three years now in our comfortable home in Lacey, Washington, surrounded by the things that remind us of our previous life overseas. We can look at the items on our shelves and remember how they came to be in our possession. Viewing those items brings back countless memories that form the comfortable reveries of our life together, and we realize how much God has blessed us.

We also seem to have come full circle in that Tim and I first started out as Peace Corps Volunteers in Malaysia in 1978. We curtailed our Peace Corps experience because I had difficulties dealing with the culture shock and sexual harassment I experienced on a daily basis. I also faced insurmountable tasks required for my job, which was to teach English to blind young adults, who ranged from those with no English background at all to those at the college prep level. To make matters worse, I didn't know Braille, and I couldn't use visual aids because my students were blind. There was no money for books, so everything for the six hours of classes six days a week had to come out of my head. I became overwhelmed at some point, so I chose the "flight" escape route and decided to leave Malaysia and the Peace Corps.

For the next eight years I beat myself up for my inability to adapt and do the job. It wasn't until I talked with the director of the English program at the small college in Lewiston, Idaho that I discovered I had been unsuccessful for many reasons, many of them not of my doing. I wasn't a quitter after all. Thirty years later, we returned to that part of the world and lived in Indonesia from 2008-2010. In a sense, returning to S.E. Asia redeemed us from our previous, unsuccessful experience. There's something comforting about completing the circle.

Tim has also been contemplating questions about God's will for our lives and recently came across two verses from Proverbs, which seem very relevant to where we are today: *"To man belong the plans of the heart, but from the Lord comes the reply of the tongue."* (Proverbs 16:1 NIV); and *"In his heart a man plans his course, but the Lord determines his steps."* (Proverbs 16:9 NIV)

I believe that if we follow God and remain in communication with Him, He will determine our steps. I believe that God wants us to lean into the questions of life but not to expect any direct revelations that will illuminate the path before us. I believe in the verse which says, *"We live by faith, not by sight."* (2 Corinthians 5:7 NIV)

If we, as fallible human beings, can understand the infinite wisdom of God and His unsearchable mysteries, then the God we worship is too small a god. We need to believe in an omnipotent, omniscient God and reconcile ourselves to possibly never understanding how everything works together. I believe in the words of the Prophet Isaiah, which reassure me: *"For my thoughts are not your thoughts, neither are your ways my ways,"* declares the Lord. *"As the heavens are higher than the earth, so are my ways higher than your ways and my thoughts than your thoughts."* (Isaiah 55:8-9 NIV) It's enough for me to believe that my Lord has drawn me with loving kindness. He has reassured me, *"And we know that in all things God works for the good of those who love him, who have been called according to his purpose."* (Romans 8:28 NIV)

I'm still trying to be the thread that follows the needle as I live out God's will for me in this tapestry we call life. As I look back, I can see some patterns emerge on the frame as my stitches are added to the weaving, together with others' whose stitches are intertwined with mine. I try not to pull away from Him and to become all tangled in the process, necessitating that my stitch be pulled out so it can be put back in the right place. He is weaving a beautiful and colorful tapestry from my tangled threads. What the finished tapestry will reveal, I don't at this point know. Although I cannot see the finished tapestry, I can see how my stitch adds a bit of color and texture to the myriad stitches from everyone else. Ultimately, I have concluded that my role as a human in God's Divine Drama, or tapestry if you prefer, is to follow the words of the Prophet Micah, *"...And what does the Lord require of you? To act justly and to love mercy and to walk humbly with your God."* (Micah 6:8 NIV) That command comforts me and quiets the questions of my heart.

Glossary

1. anak – Indonesian for child
2. becaks – Indonesian for motorized three-wheeled carts
3. chowkidar – Urdu for guard
4. cook bearer – A Pakistani cook who also cleans the house
5. dhobi – Urdu for laundryman
6. dhurries – Flat-weave wool rugs
7. domba – Indonesian for sheep
8. Eid – The Islamic celebration after a month of fasting during the month of Ramadan
9. falafel – A patty of fried chickpeas
10. galabiyya – The Egyptian garment worn by both women and men
11. il hamdu'illah – The Islamic phrase for thanks be to God
12. jalan tikus – Indonesian for a shortcut or "mouse street"
13. Khamsin – A period of 50 days where dust storms are frequent in Egypt
14. madrassa – An Islamic school for boys
15. mali – Urdu word for gardener and sweeper
16. mashribeyya – The Arabic word for a latticework screen made of carved pegs
17. memsahib – Urdu honorific for an older or foreign woman
18. Mujahideen – Rebel or fighter in Afghanistan or Pakistan
19. padi – Indonesian word for rice growing in a rice field
20. purdah – Islamic word for secluding women within the confines of their home
21. Ramadan – The month-long period of fasting from sunrise to sunset in Islam
22. shalwar kameez – A baggy garment consisting of a long tunic top and baggy trousers for women
23. shalwar kurta – A long tunic top and baggy trousers worn by men in Pakistan and Afghanistan
24. shamiana – A colorful, appliqued tent used for ceremonies or celebrations in Pakistan